DENTIST TO CEO

The Blueprint for Breaking Free from Associate Life

CHRIS K. VANDIFORD

Contents

Prologue: Where Ownership Begins ... **7**

PART I: THE OWNERSHIP MINDSET
Foundational chapters that provide the framework to shift from associate to CEO.

Chapter 1: From Associate to CEO – Your Awakening ... **12**

Chapter 2: The Five Traits That Define a Dental CEO ... **20**

PART II: CONTRACTS AND CROSSROADS
The chapters that uncover traps, highlight opportunities, and outline your next move.

Chapter 3: Read the Fine Print – Navigating Associate Contracts ... **32**

Chapter 4: The DSO (Dental Support Organization) Decision – A Bridge or a Destination? ... **45**

Chapter 5: Landing Your Dream Salary – The First Step Toward Ownership ... **54**

PART III: THE NUMBERS THAT BUILD WEALTH
Financial X-rays that reveal the true health of a practice.

Chapter 6: The Essential Metrics for Practice Valuations ... **66**

Chapter 7: Building on the Fundamentals – How to Spot Growth and Upside in a Practice ... **79**

PART IV: FROM RISK TO REWARD—MASTERING THE DEAL
Detecting risks, securing financing, and protecting goodwill.

Chapter 8: Reading the P&L Like a Detective ... 92

Chapter 9: Red Flags and Deal Breakers ... 104

Chapter 10: Smart Financing Without the Stress ... 121

PART V: WINNING HEARTS, NOT JUST NUMBERS
The trust, goodwill, and human connection that make or break a deal.

Chapter 11: Protecting the Asset You Can't Replace: Seller Goodwill ... 136

Chapter 12: Leading Like a CEO - Preserving Goodwill with Patients, Staff, and Community ... 152

PART VI: BUILDING YOUR EMPIRE
The playbook for leading, scaling, and sustaining success.

Chapter 13: Survival and Systems—The First 365 Days ... 166

Chapter 14: Growth Without Burnout ... 181

Epilogue: Your CEO Future Starts Now ... 195

Author's Note ... 197

Appendix: Tools, Templates & Checklists ... 198

Glossary and Key Concepts ... 201

Acknowledgements ... 206

About the Author ... 208

Prologue:
Where Ownership Begins

If you're an associate reading this, you know exactly what I am talking about.

It's 6:47 AM. You're in the parking lot, scrolling through today's schedule and dreading the triple-book at 2 PM. Charts are piled on your desk. Yesterday's notes still aren't finished. You should feel proud. You've hit production for eleven straight months, your patients love you, and the owner keeps saying you're the best associate he's ever had.

So why does it feel like you're running on a treadmill someone else controls? Because you are.

You bring in the collections. You calm the angry patients. You stay late, cover emergencies, and carry the rising-star label everywhere you go. You're valuable. No one disputes that.

But here's what no one tells you: **value without ownership is glorified labor.**

It doesn't matter how often your boss compliments you. It doesn't matter if you're the top producer in the practice. If your name isn't on the paperwork, every crown you prep, every late night you donate, every problem you solve, that effort compounds. Just not for you.

This feeling isn't unique to you. Nearly every associate dentist lives with it, whether they admit it or not. The difference is what happens next.

Five years from now, you'll be in one of two places.

Door one: You're still an associate. The pay is decent. The schedule is someone else's. You've watched three colleagues buy practices while you waited for the "right time." The owner is talking about selling to a DSO. You're forty-one, and you're starting over.

Door two: You own the chair. The hygiene schedule prints money while you sleep. You took a risk that terrified you, and now you're building equity instead of borrowing against your future. Your kids will inherit something real.

Same license. Same hands. Same four years of dental school. Different decision.

Dentistry is one of the few professions where a single choice can change everything. You already have the skill. You already have the license. You already have the work ethic. What you don't have yet is ownership.

This book will show you how to get it.

By the final chapter, you'll know how to:

- Read a P&L like a detective and spot the lies sellers tell themselves.

- Negotiate like you've done this before, because after you read this book, mentally, you have.

- Finance the deal without draining your savings or your sanity.

- Lead a team that doesn't need you in the room, so ownership means freedom, not a second job.

Most associates will read this prologue, nod, and never act. A few will decide that today is the day they stop building someone else's legacy.

Everything changes when they do.

PART I:
THE OWNERSHIP MINDSET

Chapter 1:
From Associate to CEO – Your Awakening

Mindset Shift: Being "valuable" is not the same as being free.

The Wake-Up Call

Dr. Elise was everything a practice owner could ask for: bright, compassionate, clinically brilliant. She hit her numbers. Her patients loved her. The staff called her "the real boss." For five years, she carried the practice on her back while the owner took extended vacations.

One afternoon, after back-to-back crown preps and an emergency root canal, she got called into the office. The owner sat casually behind the desk, sipping coffee from a mug that read: "I built this."

"Hey," he said. "You're doing great. Just wanted to say thanks for holding it down this week. I needed that time off."

And just like that, the moment hit her. She had built his dream.

Built his schedule. Built his equity. But what had she built for herself?

That day, she didn't just finish her shift….she woke up.

Two Paths, Two Futures

Every associate eventually faces the same fork in the road.

Path A: The Associate Treadmill

- Paycheck

- Ceiling

- Dependence

Path B: The CEO Runway

- Ownership

- Equity

- Freedom

Financial Reality Check #1:
The 10-Year Wealth Gap

Consider two dentists who graduate from the same school, possess identical skills, and begin their careers in the same year. One chooses to remain an associate, earning $225,000 per year with a standard 3% annual raise. The other takes the leap into ownership, earning $250,000 per year with a 10%

annual increase in income driven by scaling operations and paying down debt. The practice owner builds approximately $100,000 in equity each year through principal paydown and practice growth (see chart below).

10-Year Wealth Gap	Associate	Owner	Difference
Net Income Over 10 Years	$2.5 M	$3.9 M	+ $1.4 M
Equity Accumulated Over 10 Years	$0	$1.0 M	+ $1.0 M
Cumulative Wealth Over 10 Years	$2.5 M	$4.9 M	+ $2.4 M

Translation: Choosing the "safe" route as an associate can cost you approximately $240,000 annually in wealth potential.

In dentistry, effort alone isn't the key to success—ownership is what truly pays off. Every year you hesitate to embrace ownership is another year spent funding someone else's future instead of building your own.

Why Smart Dentists Stay Stuck

If the math is this clear, why do so many associates never make the leap?

Because the treadmill is comfortable. The paycheck arrives every two weeks. Someone else handles payroll, HR, and the broken sterilizer. You get to focus on teeth, which is what you trained for.

And underneath the comfort of the paycheck, there's fear. What if I buy a bad practice? What if I can't make payroll? What if I'm a great clinician but a terrible business owner? What if I fail and lose everything?

But here's what your brain doesn't calculate: the risk of not acting. Every year you wait, you're not standing still you're falling behind. The owner is building equity. You're building their equity. The gap widens whether you notice it or not.

Staying "safe" is its own kind of gamble. You're betting that the owner won't sell to a DSO. That your job will always be there. That you'll be satisfied at fifty doing the same thing you did at thirty, in a practice you'll never own.

That's not safety. That's risk dressed up as stability.

The Ownership Mindset

The shift from associate to owner isn't primarily financial. It's psychological.

Associates think: How do I maximize my paycheck?

Owners think: How do I build something that pays me whether I'm there or not?

Associates think: I hope they give me a raise.

Owners think: What would make this practice worth more next year than it is today?

Associates think: I'm too busy to learn the business side.

Owners think: The business side is the only thing that compounds.

This isn't about working harder. Elise was already working harder than her boss. It's about redirecting the energy you're already spending toward something you actually own. You don't need to become a different person. You need to make a different decision and then learn the skills that make that decision pay off.

That's what the rest of this book is for.

Life Lesson: The Night I Bet on Myself

I need to tell you something about myself, because you should know who's guiding you through this.

Years ago, I was driving home from a job that looked impressive on paper but left me hollow every single day. I had a wife, two young kids, and almost nothing in savings. I was forty-one years old, and I had spent a decade generating value for other people while my own future stood still.

That night, gripping the steering wheel, I did the math on my life the same way Elise did on hers. And I didn't like what I saw. I had $11,000 in the bank. No safety net. What I had was a business idea I'd built on a spreadsheet obsessively for six months, a borrowed book on practice valuations, and a wife who believed in me more than I believed in myself. I quit the next week.

The first year was brutal. I made mistakes that cost me sleep and money. I learned things about leadership, negotiation, and finance that a college degree never mentioned. Some nights I wondered if I'd destroyed my family's security for an ego trip. But I owned what I was building. For the first time, the effort began to compound for me.

15 years later, I've helped hundreds of dentists make that same bet to stop renting their potential and start owning their future. Some bought small practices in rural towns. Some acquired multi-location operations in competitive cities. All of them faced the same fears you're facing now.

This book is the roadmap I wish I'd had on that drive home.

Executive Summary

1. **Value without ownership has a ceiling.** You can be the top producer in the practice and still build nothing for yourself. If your name isn't on the paperwork, the effort compounds for someone else.

2. **The "safe" path carries its own risk.** Staying an associate feels secure until the owner sells to a DSO, the buy-in never materializes, or you're fifty and starting over. Comfort isn't the same as safety.

3. **The gap is math, not motivation.** Over ten years, the wealth difference between associate and owner can exceed $2 million—same skills, same hours, different decision.

4. **Ownership is a choice, not a promotion.** No one hands you equity. If the path to ownership isn't written in ink, it doesn't exist. Stop waiting for permission and start building the knowledge to act.

Action Plan: From Associate to CEO – Your Awakening

1. Name the gap. Write down the single biggest obstacle keeping you from ownership (time, fear, debt, knowledge). Quantify its cost in lost freedom or wealth.

____

____

____

2. Make a CEO decision this week. Make one concrete move that shifts you from employee-to-owner thinking: start a savings account labeled "Equity Fund," schedule a call with a broker, or map out your five-year acquisition goal.

____

____

____

3. Reframe risk. List one risk that you've avoided that an owner would embrace. What's the upside you've been protecting yourself from?

____

____

____

CEO Toolkit

Download the Associate-to-CEO Starter Kit—including the Equity Gap Calculator, Career Path Self-Assessment, and Ownership Readiness Checklist at: *www.TransitionOne.net/ DentistToCEO/Toolkit*

Chapter 2:
The Five Traits
That Define a Dental CEO

Mindset Shift: Every breakthrough begins with breaking out of the limits you've outgrown. Abandon the role you've played too long, and let go of the fears that no longer serve you.

The Inner Battle

Every dentist fights two battles: one with the handpiece, and one in their head. The first is clinical. The second is invisible—fear of risk, rejection, and being "not ready."

Dr. Maya Chen fought that second battle for years. She was a brilliant clinician and loyal associate. Then one Friday, her schedule fell apart. Three cancellations and two emergencies later, she found herself managing a frantic office while the owner enjoyed a day off. The realization hit hard: she was already carrying the risk and stress of a dental practice—without the compensation or equity.

That night, Maya applied for loan preapproval to finance her own practice. She was ready to take ownership – and that decision changed everything.

The difference between dentists who stay stuck and those who scale has less to do with clinical skill and more to do with cultivating leadership traits.

The Five Traits Ladder

The Five Traits Ladder illustrates how each of these essential traits functions as a rung, elevating you toward freedom, ownership, and impact. If you skip a rung, you risk stalling. Master all five, and you will ascend to new heights. Every dental CEO I have encountered embodies these five crucial traits that transform clinical expertise into enterprise value.

1. Vision:
Seeing beyond the chair

Dr. Erin crafted her five-year plan before even purchasing her first practice. With a clear goal of ownership by age 30, she strategically outlined the necessary steps: pay off debt, save $200K, and find a practice with over 2,000 active patients. In stark contrast, the vast majority of associates focus solely on the immediate demands of Friday's schedule, whereas successful CEOs think five years ahead. Without a vision, you risk becoming an unwitting participant in someone else's plan.

2. Courage:
Taking on risks when others freeze

Courage is the ability to take calculated risks, even when those around you freeze in fear. Dr. Maya Chen left a seemingly secure associate position earning $225K a year, despite the chorus of naysayers who labeled her decision as reckless. However, the practice she acquired doubled her income within two years. Many dentists find themselves paralyzed by student loan debt, but true courage is not about being rash; it involves making strategic choices in the face of fear. Without courage, you may never break free from the cycle of associate roles.

3. Discipline:
Doing what others won't

Discipline is about doing what others won't. Dr. Alicia drove a ten-year-old Honda while her friends opted for luxury BMW leases. She packed her lunches while others financed vacations. By age 32, she had amassed the funds to buy her first practice outright. Discipline is what transforms vision into reality; without it, your dreams remain mere fantasies. It's the foundation upon which ownership is built.

4. Influence:
Winning people, not just producing dentistry

Influence is about winning people over rather than merely producing dentistry. Begin by fostering influence within your current team and embrace leadership in your associate role today. Dr. Sam acquired a practice with a high staff turnover rate. Instead of imposing immediate changes, he dedicated the first three months to listening and investing in his employees. A decade later, nearly all of those original staff members remain with him. If a dental CEO cannot effectively lead their team, patient retention will suffer. Without influence, your staff will become disengaged, and your patients will not stay.

5. Resilience:
Rising again when deals or dreams collapse

Resilience is the ability to rise again after deals or dreams falter. Dr. Maria faced a significant setback when she lost her first practice deal at the closing table. Rather than retreating, she leveraged the lessons learned and refined her financial acumen. Just six months later, she successfully acquired a more promising practice and now mentors other aspiring buyers. Resilience is not simply about enduring failure; it's about refusing to let it define your identity. These traits are not optional; they are the daily choices and behaviors that are essential for success.

CEO Insight—The ROI of Traits

Vision → Predicts five years in advance, not five patients ahead. This is how strategy replaces stress.

Courage → Commits to the loan others are afraid to sign—and doubles income in two years.

Discipline → Packs lunch, drives the old car, buys freedom early.

Influence → Develops teams that remain loyal, patients that refer, and a culture of ownership.

Resilience → Transforms a failed deal into a better one after six months.

Bottom Line: Skills build production. Traits build empires.

These traits divide the dentists who keep waiting for "someday" from the ones who own it now. No story illustrates that contrast—or the cost of waiting—better than Dr. Adrian, the dentist who waited too long.

CEO Story:
The Dentist Who Waited Too Long

Dr. Adrian was everyone's favorite associate—12 years in, $280K salary, respected by patient and staff. But every New Year's brought the same response:

"Someday I'll buy a practice."

"Someday when the kids are older."

"Someday when I'm more ready."

Then the phone call came. The owner had sold to a DSO. Overnight, his job became a high-stress contract. His autonomy vanished. His pay dropped. Staff turnover surged.

He didn't lose because he was lazy. He lost because he waited.

The Hidden Cost of Playing Small

Staying safe has a price tag, and it's far higher than most dentists realize. Every year you postpone ownership, the following truths unfold:

- Self-Assurance: You begin doubting your potential instead of developing it.

- Freedom: You give your time, talent, and vision to someone else's priorities.

- Momentum: Comfort calcifies. Before long, your ambition softens and your skills plateau.

The truth? Playing small isn't cheap. It costs so much energy, identity, and the belief that you were made for more. Whenever you postpone the next step—ownership, leadership or risk— you reinforce the idea that now isn't the time. But waiting does not make you any better prepared. It only makes you feel you should wait a little longer.

Comfort compounds like interest, but in reverse. And with every year you play it safe, you're quietly paying the tax of unrealized potential—meanwhile, the dentists who took imperfect action built equity, self-confidence, and freedom.

The more time you wait for certainty, the more expensive the waiting is.

Financial Reality Check #2: The Cost of Waiting

Two dentists. Same school. Same debt. Same skills. But one leaps now, and the other waits three years "until the time feels right."

10-Year Wealth Gap	Dr. A – Buys a Practice Now	Dr. B – Waits 3 Years
Years of Ownership	10 Years	7 Years
Net Income Over 10 Years	$3.9 M	$3.0 M
Equity Accumulated Over 10 Years	$1.0 M	$0.7 M
Cumulative Wealth Over 10 Years	$4.9 M	$3.7 M
Cost of Waiting 3 Years		= $1.2 M Lost

*Assumes associate earns $225,000 per year with a standard 3% annual raise. Owner earns $250,000 per year with a 10% annual increase. Furthermore, practice owner builds approximately $100,000 in equity each year.

*Net income refers to actual take-home earnings after expense payments and service on debt—not gross production or collections.

Life Lesson: From Burned-Out to Bought-In

Dr. Alex was the ultimate "clinical guy," a perfectionist who lived for his patients. The associate job seemed perfect: good pay, modern office and no business headaches. But six years in, the shine faded from the job. Assistants turned over. His boss's decisions on patient care clashed with his values. Treatment plans were scrutinized not by patients, but by a front desk with quotas to achieve. The final blow? Training a junior associate who was then promoted over him.

That week I received a call from Alex: "I'm not building any-thing. I'm just maintaining someone else's success."

The shift was quiet but seismic. It did not happen overnight, but it transformed everything that followed. He began small: tracking his production, studying potential overhead, and reading business books between lunch breaks. At first, he was not planning to leave; he was looking to grow. When a retiring dentist offered her practice, Alex hesitated. The numbers were daunting, but staying stuck was worse. He bought it.

The first year included chaos, missed projections, staffing conflicts and sleepless nights. But six months in, something clicked: "The wins are mine. The failures are mine. And both are making me better."

The Greatest ROI: You

The best investment you'll ever make isn't a new Cone Beam, CE course, mentor or miracle; it's your mindset. How you view risk, along with time and yourself, will dictate how far you go. Every decision you make now influences the CEO you will become.

So will you keep building someone else's dream, or will you

finally build your own? Because the highest return on investment isn't financial—it's personal.

Take a breath before you turn the page. You've read about the traits that define every successful dental CEO—vision, courage, discipline, influence, and resilience. Now ask yourself: **Which one will define your first year of ownership?**

Executive Summary

1. **Identity is the starting point.** You don't need a loan or a title to think like a CEO. Start before you're ready.

2. **Mindset is the multiplier.** How you consider risk, time, and value determines how far you will go.

3. **Discomfort can point you in the right direction.** The path that makes you uncomfortable is usually the one that will help you grow. You will naturally be cautious while taking a risk.

4. **Leadership starts before ownership.** You don't become a leader after you sign a lease. You become a leader when you begin to make decisions that represent the future you're building.

5. **You are the asset.** Stop seeing yourself as a producer. Start looking at yourself as the architect of your future.

Action Plan: The Five Traits That Define a Dental CEO

1. Rate Your Traits. Score yourself 1 to 10 in each of the five CEO traits: Vision, Courage, Discipline, Influence, Resilience. Be honest; awareness is your baseline for growth.

2.

    Vision –

    Courage –

    Discipline –

    Influence –

    Resilience –

    Identify growth opportunities. Pick the one trait in which you gave yourself the lowest score. How will you plan to improve this one area?

    ____

    ____

    ____

3. Design a 30-Day Plan. Create one specific step to strengthen that trait: read a leadership book, join a mastermind group, track morning discipline, or practice one courageous conversation per week.

    ____

    ____

    ____

4. Leverage your strengths. Think about the two traits you're well versed in. Do not let this go unexplained; these were the only two of them you scored highest. What do you do with them to help foster your weakest area. Take this example: disciplined action builds courage.

____

____

____

5. Document the shift. At the end of the month, write a little reflection: "When I chose to focus on CEO traits instead of production metrics, what has changed in the way that I decide?" That thought then serves as your first CEO progress report.

____

____

____

CEO Toolkit

Download the CEO Blueprint Planner—a guided worksheet to design your ideal practice, define your Freedom Metrics, and map the next 3 moves that turn clarity into ownership at _www.TransitionOne.net/DentistToCEO/Toolkit_

PART II: CONTRACTS AND CROSSROADS

Chapter 3:
Read the Fine Print – Navigating Associate Contracts

Mindset Shift: Your signature can shape or sabotage your future.

The Trap in Plain Sight

Dr. Kayla thought she was set. The office was busy, the team was friendly, the pay was fair. Then she signed a contract with an assignable 15-mile noncompete clause. When the owner sold to a DSO (Dental Support Organization) for a high price, Kayla had no leverage. The employment terms were transferable, including the restrictive-covenant mileage. She couldn't buy in, couldn't open nearby, couldn't practice in her own hometown. Overnight, a decade of loyalty became worthless. One signature had boxed her out of her future.

Contracts aren't just paperwork. They're handcuffs or keys. Ignore the fine print, and you might be building someone else's dream while locking yourself out of your own.

Why Associates Get Burned

Most associates skim contracts for salary and gloss over the rest—or worse, sign without reading. But contracts aren't written to protect you; they're written to protect the owner.

Your job as a future CEO? Read them like a detective. Spot the traps. Know when to push back. And walk away when the deal kills your future.

CEO Insight—The Three Truths of Every Deal

Everything is negotiable, especially timelines and terms.

The first draft always favors the writer.

Silence at the table is often your most profitable move.

The Five Contract Landmines

Imagine navigating every associate contract as if it were a field of hidden landmines—step out of line, and the repercussions could surface years later.

The Career Cage: Noncompete Clauses

- **The Trap:** Restrictions of 10–20 miles and 3–5 years, often blacking out entire counties.

- **Case Study:** Dr. Tim signed a 20-mile noncompete. When he changed jobs, his only option was a two-hour commute—turning a "good contract" into a daily punishment.

- **Survival Rule:** Never sign a clause you wouldn't be comfortable living with. Aim for limits of 5–10 miles in urban areas and 15 miles in rural settings.

Notice Periods: The Golden Handcuffs

- **The Trap:** A seemingly benign "120-day notice required" can become a burden when you›re unhappy and trapped for four months.

- **Case Study:** Dr. Kayla gave notice and learned it meant four more months in a hostile office—proof that long notice periods aren't professional, they're punitive.

- **Survival Rule:** Keep notice periods to a maximum of 30–60 days. Anything longer is just a leash.

Automatic Renewals: The Hidden Contract

- **The Trap:** Often buried in fine print: "Renews automatically unless terminated 90 days prior." Miss this deadline, and you could be locked in for another year.

- **Case Study:** Dr. Ben overlooked the renewal window and found himself tied to a toxic office for an additional three years due to a single signature.

- **Survival Rule:** Eliminate automatic renewals. Contracts should end unless you choose to renew.

Punitive Clauses: The Silent Killers

- **The Trap:** Clauses that penalize you by docking pay, cutting bonuses, or imposing penalties for leaving.

- **Case Study:** Dr. Nina lost a $20,000 bonus when she resigned—hidden in the contract as a "training reimbursement."

- **Survival Rule:** If a clause feels punitive, it likely is. Walk away.

Unclear Bonus Structures: The Mirage

- **The Trap:** Promises of "production bonuses," "profit sharing," or "quarterly incentives" that lack clear written terms. If it's vague, it's illusory.

- **Case Study:** Dr. Alex was promised 20% over a collections target, but the target was never defined. After two years, he had not earned a penny.

- **Survival Rule:** If a bonus isn't documented in black and white—complete with numbers, formulas, and timelines—it doesn't exist.

The 3+ Rule: If You See Three or More Red Flags, Walk Away

The perfect contract doesn't exist, but contracts can help you detect potential poison. One bad clause can be negotiated. Two may be fixable. Three or more? That's not a practice. That's a trap.

Why Contracts Matter More Than Pay

Salary can often blind young dentists. The allure of a $225K salary might prompt an immediate decision: "I'll sign right now." But let's consider an essential truth:

- A salary lasts a year.

- Contract terms last five.

What good is a $225K salary if it restricts your ability to practice in your own city when you leave? The right contract can accelerate your journey toward ownership. A fair contract not only protects both parties but also fosters growth and positions you as a leader, even before you've signed a loan.

Here are the four pillars of an associate contract designed to guide you along the path to ownership:

1. **A Clear Path to Partnership**

- **The Win:** A written timeline, a transparent method for valuation, and the first right of refusal.

- **Case Study:** Dr. Anna's contract included a five-year buy-in plan with her valuation set at 65% of collections. When the time came for her transition, there were no surprises, and she moved seamlessly into equity.

- **Importance:** Without clarity, you risk merely being a producer. With it, you're already on the road to ownership.

2. **Built-In Mentorship**

- **The Win:** A commitment to regular mentorship, including monthly reviews and leadership training.

- **Case Study:** Dr. Mark's mentor clause required quarterly meetings with the owner. These sessions equipped him with essential skills in staff management and financial analysis—tools that nearly doubled his confidence in handling a future purchase.

- **Importance:** Ownership extends beyond numbers; it demands leadership. A mentor ensures you learn the business while practicing dentistry.

3. **Defined and Transparent Compensation**

- **The Win:** A clear pay structure, with bonuses tied to growth metrics such as case acceptance, collections, or new patients.

- **Case Study:** Dr. Lisa's contract stipulated 30% of adjusted production and included a bonus for a 10% increase in case acceptance from the previous year. This approach eliminated confusion and resentment, fostering trust and providing additional income for her ownership goals.

- **Importance:** Clarity builds trust. It secures current income and enables you to reverse-engineer your preparedness for the future.

4. **Reasonable Noncompete and Seller Support**

- **The Win:** A noncompete clause that is limited to the office where you work, along with a commitment from the seller for support.

- **Case Study:** Dr. James's contract featured a short noncompete radius and a clause ensuring the seller would mentor him while transitioning patients within the company. This arrangement maintained loyalty and allowed James to step into his new role without losing goodwill.

- **Importance:** An overly restrictive noncompete signals fear. A fair contract illustrates a genuine investment in your future.

Conclusion: Contracts Are Your Safety Net

Not every contract is a trap. The best contracts protect you now and pave the way for future equity.

Read the fine print—it's your opportunity to prove you're ready to lead. If you can't assert yourself against a contract, how will you stand firm against a bank, a seller, or a landlord?

This is your first true choice for ownership, so make it count.

CEO Story: The Contract that Created a CEO

When Dr. Allie graduated, her classmates signed whatever was handed to them. She didn't. Her mentor told her, "The contract is your future, treat it like ownership training."

So, she pushed back on three things before signing:

1. **Fair pay**: 32% of collections with clear monthly reporting

2. **Short notice**: 45 days, so she wouldn't miss out on ownership opportunities

3. **Buy-in Option**: If the practice ever went up for sale, she was offered first right of refusal.

At first, she worried she was asking for too much. But the owner respected her for negotiating like a leader. Eighteen months later, that clause changed everything. The seller decided to retire, and because of her contract, Allie was the first in line. No bidding war. No endless waiting. No lawyers boxing her out.

The bank looked at her production history, already $900K in annual production thanks to her fair compensation, and said "yes" in weeks. By her third year out of school, she wasn't an associate begging for time off. She was CEO of a $1.9M practice, employing two associates herself.

Her words? "That contract didn't just protect me. It handed me the keys to my future.

Contract Traps vs. CEO Clauses Summary

The difference between signing fast and signing smart isn't just in the numbers—it's in the clauses.

Every contract either protects your potential or profits from your silence. The difference comes down to the clauses you sign—or the ones you demand.

Here's what separates a regret from a reward.

Contract Trap	CEO Clause	Why it matters
Vague Ownership Promises ("We'll revisit partnership in 1–2 years.")	Written Timeline + Defined Terms ("Partnership by month 24 at X valuation formula.")	Verbal promises fade. Ink builds equity.
Ambiguous Pay Formula ("Compensation based on adjusted production.")	Clear Percentage + Defined Adjustments ("33% of collected production after lab fees.")	Transparency eliminates manipulation.
Uncapped Noncompete (10+ miles or multiple locations.)	Tight, Specific Scope (Radius limited to the actual practice zip.)	Protects your career geography.
Unilateral Termination Clause ("Employer may terminate at any time without cause.")	Mutual Exit Clause + Notice Period (Both parties require 60–90 days' notice.)	Gives you time to plan and protect your income.
Restrictive Non-Solicit (Covers all staff and patients in a multi-office group.)	Tailored to One Office / Location	Prevents career handcuffs and protects relationships.
Undefined Buy-In Price ("Valuation to be determined later.")	Pre-Agreed Formula (EBITDA × Multiple or Appraisal Method.)	Ambiguity kills deals— numbers build trust.
One-Sided Arbitration Clause (Employer picks the arbitrator or venue.)	Neutral Arbitration or Mediation Clause	Keeps disputes fair and affordable.
No Restriction on Sale (Owner can sell DSO at any time.)	Right of First Refusal	Lets you buy before outsiders do.

Executive Summary

1. **Contracts shape your future, not just your present.** A job offer is not just a head start, it's a strategic commitment. Read contracts with a leader's eye, not from desperation to get hired.

2. **Restrictive covenants = Roadblocks to careers.** That noncompete clause? It could leave you out of your dream location. Know the limits before they become landmine status.

3. **Notice periods create or destroy flexibility.** A 120-day notice might lock you out of new practice opportunities. Stand firm for the terms that protect your momentum and future.

4. **Punitive clauses expose a practices culture.** Punitive measures or vague bonus structures often signal leadership that you don't want to work under. The fine print reflects the mindset at the top.

5. **Negotiate like your future depends on it, because it does.** Ask the difficult questions. Push back when needed. Ownership begins with the resolve to speak up for yourself today.

Action Plan: Read the Fine Print – Navigating Associate Contracts

1. Audit what you've signed (or will sign). Pull your current or most recent associate contract. Highlight every clause that affects ownership potential: noncompete, notice period, renewal terms, or liquidated damages. Summarize below, including page numbers for your reference.

____

____

____

2. Spot the deal breakers. Embrace the "three strikes rule": if you find three or more restrictive clauses (broad radius, long notice, unclear bonus structure), define it as a career-limiting contract. But out of the above list, are there any deal breakers? List below.

____

____

____

3. Keep Record of your current or expected notice period. Evaluate how that timeline could impact your flexibility to pursue or close on an ownership opportunity when the right practice becomes available.

____

____

____

4. Create your non-negotiables list. Set your personal standards for all future agreements (e.g., noncompete <10 miles, notice ≤60 days, transparent bonus terms). Keep this list on file for every opportunity.

____

____

____

CEO Toolkit

Download the Associate Contract Red Flags Checklist and Negotiation Prep Worksheet to review real-world clauses and rewrite them with confidence at: *www.TransitionOne.net/DentistToCEO/Toolkit*

Chapter 4:
The DSO (Dental Support Organization) Decision – A Bridge or a Destination?

Mindset Shift: Over 30% of new grads join DSOs, but fewer than 10% stay more than two years.

The Trade-Off: Effort vs. Equity

Dr. Priya was ambitious right out of dental school and ready to prove herself. The DSO recruiter promised mentorship, steady patients, and a "fast track" to success.

What she got was 55-hour workweeks, quotas that never stopped climbing, and a paycheck that didn't match her effort. One Friday night, drowning in notes, Priya realized the truth—she was building someone else's spreadsheet. But she needed to figure out what she would build for herself.

Financial Reality Check #3: The DSO vs. Ownership Trajectory

At first glance, the DSO offer looks smart—predictable income, no loans, less pressure. But the illusion of safety hides the real cost: lost leverage and lost time.

Year	DSO Associate (Salary + Bonus)	Private Practice Owner (Net Income + Equity Growth)	Wealth Gap
1	$225 K	$250 K + $100 K equity = $350 K	+$125 K
2	$231 K	$275 K + $100 K equity = $375 K	+$143 K
3	$238 K	$302 K + $100 K equity = $402 K	+$163 K

3-Year Total:

- **DSO path:** $695K earned, $0 equity built

- **Ownership path:** $827K earned + $300K equity = **$1.1M total**

Freedom Gap after 3 years: $432K—and widening every month.

Translation: The "safe" job may match income early on, but ownership adds leverage, equity, and time control that no W-2 can match. The paycheck buys comfort; equity buys control. That's the real fast track—the one that leads to freedom.

Your income is never limited by effort. It's limited by the environment's capacity to deploy your skill.

Another Path

Now contrast that with her classmate, Dr. Andrew. Instead of signing with a DSO, he partnered with a retiring small-town dentist. Within two years, Andrew owned the practice. His hours were still long, but every crown, every hygiene recall, every patient was building his future.

Same school. Same student debt. Same skills. Two choices. Two radically different outcomes.

That's the DSO dilemma. They're not evil. They're just designed for shareholders—not associates.

The Gateway vs. The Treadmill

The Gateway Path: When treated like a bridge job, 12–24 months max, DSOs can give you income, confidence, and technical speed before ownership.

✓ Guaranteed paycheck when loans feel crushing

✓ Systems and protocols that teach efficiency

✓ Mentorship and reps in high-volume dentistry

✓ Zero ownership headaches in year one

The Treadmill Path: For others, DSOs become a trap.

▷ Quotas that prize speed over quality

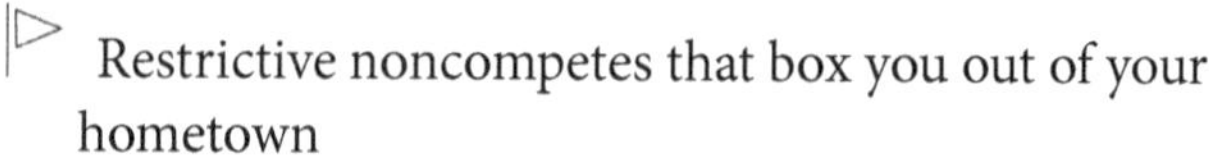

> Restrictive noncompetes that box you out of your hometown

> "Family culture" that feels more like corporate control

> Years lost producing for equity you'll never own

What was supposed to be a steppingstone became a barrier.

CEO Insight: What No One Tells You

- The bigger the signing bonus, the more they plan to own your schedule.

- If your noncompete covers more zip codes than you can count, you're not signing a contract, you're walking into a cage.

- High production numbers look great until you realize you built someone else's empire.

DSO Contract Non-Negotiables Checklist

Employment contracts at DSOs are written to protect investors. This list helps you protect yourself.

Before you sign, confirm these five items are transparent—in writing.

1. **Signing Bonus Clawback:** If you leave early, how much

do you repay, and on what timeline?

2. **Noncompete Radius:** Exact mileage and duration. A "25 miles from any location" clause can erase your city.

3. **Production Quotas:** Define daily/hourly targets and tie them to real patient flow.

4. **Schedule Control:** Can they change your hours or move you between sites without consent?

5. **Termination Rights:** Notice period for both sides; who finishes treatment?

Bottom Line: If it's not defined, it's flexible—for them, not you.

How to Use a DSO as a Launchpad

Working for a DSO doesn't have to be the end of your ownership dream—it can be the bridge that funds it. Here's how to turn the experience into your personal MBA:

1. Pay Off Debt Intentionally – Use your stable income to crush student loans and build your credit score. Every dollar of debt you clear now becomes borrowing power later.

2. Learn the Systems – Study how the DSO runs scheduling, KPIs, and HR. Take notes—you're getting a free masterclass in scalable operations.

3. Document What Works (and What Doesn't) – Keep a "Playbook" journal of their best workflows and their biggest mistakes. You'll reuse the best systems when you open your own practice.

4. Build Cash Reserves – Set aside at least six months of personal expenses and startup capital. That cushion becomes your runway to ownership.

5. Exit on Purpose – Don't just quit. Leave with relationships, referrals, and a timeline that sets you up for your next step. The goal isn't to escape—it's to evolve.

CEO Story: The Smart DSO Play

Dr. Lacey joined a regional DSO with a plan: learn leadership systems, master KPIs, and build cash. Two years later, she left with $300K in savings and the operational confidence most owners never gain. DSOs aren't the enemy—they're classrooms for future CEOs who know when to walk away.

Employment or Ownership? The Choice is Yours

At the end of the day, the DSO question isn't about good or bad. It's about who controls your future.

Your employer will always pay just enough for you to stay, but never enough to own. Once again, owning your own practice is the only path that truly builds income, equity and quality of life.

So ask yourself: Do I want to be the employee who makes someone else rich? Or the CEO who builds a future worth owning? That's not just a career decision. That's your future.

Executive Summary

1. **DSOs are not the enemy, complacency is**. Use your time at a DSO to level up. Then you can move on when it's your time to start your career.

2. **Don't sign blind**. Know your contract. Know your rights. Spot red flags before they become roadblocks.

3. **Learn the business from the inside out**. Master production, case acceptance, team dynamics, and collections. Let the DSO pay you to learn what they never taught you in school.

4. **Stack cash and build clarity**. Save aggressively. Live below your means. Exit with intention and with options.

Action Plan: The DSO (Dental Sales Organization) Decision – A Bridge or a Destination?

1. The first step could be to examine your current or prospective DSO contract. Look for clauses, specifically noncompete and termination terms, which might limit your freedom to move forward with ownership when the time comes.

____

____

____

2. Pinpoint one business skill to master. Identify one business skill that you want to become proficient in. Select one skill you can intentionally hone over the course of your tenure — such as case acceptance, leadership, or collections — that will actually prepare you for ownership

____

____

____

3. Calculate your ownership launch fund. Calculate how much cash you can realistically save over the next 12 months by living below your means while working in a DSO.

____

____

____

4. Define your exit criteria. Write down those conditions under which you know it is time to step out of the DSO—be it whether it's an individual saving target, skill score, or time span—so that when departure happens you approach it with strategy (and not emotional reaction).

CEO Toolkit

Download the DSO Strategy Playbook—your step-by-step guide to maximizing income, mastering systems, and preparing your exit to ownership—includes editable scoring tables and financial calculators at: *www.TransitionOne.net/DentistToCEO/Toolkit*

Chapter 5:
Landing Your Dream Salary – The First Step Toward Ownership

Mindset Shift: You didn't sacrifice your twenties, miss holidays with your family, and rack up six figures in student loans just to take a job that burns you out and boxes you in. Every patient conversation, every production target, every decision to stay late or speak up is either preparing you to own your future or chaining you to someone else's.

Life Lesson: "My First Boss Let Me Drown—and It Was the Best Thing That Happened"

Dr. Marcus thought he had landed his dream job. In reality, he'd just signed up for burnout.

- One chair, endless patients

- A boss who only appeared to collect profits

- A team that tossed him charts like grenades

- No mentorship, no roadmap

By the third month, Marcus was spent, uncertain of his abilities, and broke. After all that grinding, the number on his paychecks was nowhere near what he expected.

Instead of quitting, Marcus reverse-engineered the numbers. He tracked every patient, every procedure, and every line item that shaved dollars off his production. He discovered the gap between "what he produced" and "what he got paid." That's when everything shifted.

- He learned which procedures actually drove income versus which just burned his time.

- He saw how overhead and inefficiency silently killed profit.

- He realized if he didn't understand the business side, he'd always be at the mercy of someone else's math.

Fast forward: Marcus owns a thriving practice and mentors young dentists. His lesson? "Don't just work. Learn. Your first job is your business school. If you're not building skills for ownership, you're wasting your grind."

The Associate Illusion

A strong associate position teaches you how to treat patients efficiently—but it rarely teaches you how to run a business. Most owners will keep you busy, but not all procedures pay the same. If you don't set your own timeline for ownership, someone else will gladly use your talent to build theirs.

The $200K Reality Check

Want to earn $200K as an associate? Here's the math.

At 30% of collections (the industry standard):

- $200K/year = $667K in restorative collections

- $16.7K/month = $55.5K in collections

- $4.1K/week = $13.9K in collections

- $1K/day = $3.5K in collections

Translation: If the practice can't give you that opportunity, walk away. A shiny office doesn't pay student loans.

Pro Tip: Don't just chase salary. Chase environments that allow you to grow. A $150K paycheck in the right office with growth, mentorship, and CE beats $200K in a dead-end office that boxes you in.

Know the Numbers Before You Sign

Signing without asking for practice data is like diagnosing without X-rays. Key questions include:

- Average daily production for associates

- How many hygiene patients per day? (10–12 = strong diagnostic flow)

- Will I get new patients?

- What procedures are referred out? (opportunity to keep revenue in-house)

- How many full-time hygienists? (3+ means you'll stay busy)

If they dodge, that's your answer. Transparency = confidence.

Systems Decide Your Success

A great practice multiplies your effort. A weak one grinds you down. Look for:

- Assistant-to-doctor ratio: At least one dedicated assistant. Two = gold.

- Digital systems: X-rays, charting, scheduling—modern and smooth.

- Patient recall protocols: A strong reappointment system = a full chair.

Without systems, you'll be working twice as hard for half the result.

Sidebar: Owner Promises vs. Reality

When you're interviewing for an associate role, listen closely. Sellers rarely lie outright, but they often "frame" the truth. Here's how it usually plays out:

Owner: "You'll be busy from day one. We're bursting at the seams."
Reality: You'll be busy with *what*? Bread-and-butter fillings? Low-value procedures? Or is there actually patient demand for high-value dentistry? "Busy" doesn't always mean "profitable."

Owner: "You'll have the chance to buy in eventually."
Reality: Without a written timeline, valuation method, and first right of refusal, "eventually" = never. If it's not in ink, it's fiction.

Owner: "We have a very loyal patient base."
Reality: Most of those patients are loyal to *me,* not you. Unless I endorse you personally and help with the transition, loyalty doesn't transfer automatically.

Owner: "Compensation is fair."
Reality: Fair by whose definition? If it's below 30% of collections or has vague bonus structures, you're already set up to lose.

Stand Out and Win the Right Job

- Tailor your outreach: Send a professional letter and photo to every dentist in your area of interest. $40 in stamps could change your career.

- Monitor your production: Measure daily numbers from day one. You can count on the numbers to show whether the problem is you—or the system.

- Build staff trust: Respect the assistants and front desk. They'll make you or break you.

- Invest in high-value skills: Endo, implants, sedation— these give you current and unstoppable power tomorrow.

Pro Tip: The Associate ROI Formula: Income + Learning + Mentorship – Burnout = True ROI

Growth Strategy: Associate Compensation Benchmark (12 Months In)

At the one-year mark, here's what a thriving associate should look like:

- Monthly Production: $60,000–$70,000 → A fully ramped associate, working a full schedule with strong patient flow

- Annual Production: $720,000–$840,000 → A sizable revenue contributor, often ready for ownership or partnership discussions

- Collections: 98% of production ($58,800–$68,600/month) → Normal insurance adjustments applied, showing real dollars hitting the bank

- Compensation: 30% of collections ($17,600–$20,500/month) → Commission-based income bracket for high-performing associates

- Annual Income: $211,000–$246,000 → What a "12-month-in" thriving associate is paid under regular models

Why it matters: These benchmarks indicate you're read to succeed. Hit them, and you're setting yourself up for ownership readiness and demonstrating financial management. If you fall short, you've spotted the gaps that need closing before you jump.

CEO Insight: If you're a year in and you're not producing $60K+ on a 4-day-a-weekwork schedule, ask yourself (or better yet, ask the owner of the business), how you can improve the systems to enable you to work more efficiently. Don't just work harder; fix the systems, the schedule, or the support. Income follows production, but production follows structure.

The Launch Plan

1. Stay two years max unless a written buy-in exists.

2. Use those years to build speed, cash flow, and confidence.

3. When you hit clinical competence and financial readiness, start your search for ownership.

Every month you stay beyond that window without a contractual path, you're funding someone else's equity.

CEO Insight: High performers don't chase paychecks. They choose platforms. If an office can't give you the volume, reps, and headroom to grow, the salary is irrelevant. Great careers are built where capacity meets ambition.

Executive Summary

1. **Your first job is your launchpad**. This isn't just about earning a paycheck; it's your training ground for leadership. Every procedure, every patient conversation, and every production goal is preparing you to one day run your own practice.

2. **Reverse-engineer your paycheck**. To hit a $200K income, you'll need to collect about $667K annually. Anything less? You're on a treadmill, not a track to ownership.

3. **Know the numbers or get burned**. If you're not asking about average production, hygiene flow, and new patient counts, you're setting yourself up for disappointment.

Transparency is non-negotiable.

4. **Culture and mentorship matter**. A supportive environment accelerates your growth. A toxic one stunts it. Ask about mentorship, assistant support, and practice systems. If they're missing, keep moving.

5. **Don't just work; build value and track your production**. Sharpen your skills. Invest in procedures like implants or endo. Everything you learn now increases your future equity and your freedom.

Action Plan: Landing Your Dream Salary – The First Step Toward Ownership

1. Evaluate the true launch potential. Review your current or potential job. Does it offer mentorship, transparency, and room for leadership, or just production pressure? Write down three factors that make it a launchpad, not a dead end.

____

____

____

2. Run the math on your paycheck. Reverse-engineer your income target. Start with your desired **annual income**, divide by **0.30** to find required annual production. Then divide by **220 working days** to calculate the **daily production target** you must consistently hit.

____

____

3. Ask for the numbers that matter. Before signing, request data on the practice's average daily production, hygiene patient flow, and new patient counts. If the answers aren't clear, neither is your future. Identify the most important numbers you need before signing a job offer (production averages, hygiene flow, new patients). Write them down.

____

____

____

4. Map your first-year growth plan. Identify one high-value clinical or leadership skill (implants, endo, communication, case presentation) you'll master over the next 12 months that increases your ownership value. Write that goal below with a step-by-step plan of how you will learn it.

____

____

____

5. Track and reflect quarterly. Create a personal Associate Scorecard measuring production, patient flow, and learning milestones. Use it to determine when you've outgrown your current position and are ready to own.

____

____

____

CEO Toolkit

Download the Associate Launchpad Planner—a guided worksheet to reverse-engineer your ideal income, evaluate job offers with real metrics, and identify the skills that accelerate your path to ownership at: *www.TransitionOne.net/DentistToCEO/Toolkit*

PART III:
THE NUMBERS THAT BUILD WEALTH

Chapter 6:
The Essential Metrics for Practice Valuations

Mindset Shift: Too many dentists buy practices based on emotion, not fundamentals. But real CEOs do it the other way around. Every great business, dental or otherwise, is built on numbers. Not guesses. Not gut feelings. Numbers.

What you will master in this chapter:

1. Identify the heartbeat of a practice by measuring active patients and why that number matters more than shiny equipment or location.

2. Calculate cost per patient to instantly spot underpriced or overpriced practices.

3. Apply the 400-patient rule to determine how many doctor days a practice can sustain.

4. Project revenue potential with precision so you can uncover hidden upside others miss.

This isn't accounting trivia. These are the numbers that make or break million-dollar decisions.

Life Lesson: The $900K Near Mistake

I'll never forget Dr. Lisa, a sharp, ambitious associate who was hungry to own her first practice. She found what looked like a dream listing: a sleek, urban office with $1 million in annual collections and a $900,000 price tag. The seller talked it up like it was a goldmine: modern chairs, fancy tech, and a "loyal" patient base.

But before she signed, I asked a simple question: "Have you run the numbers?"

We popped the hood.

Red Flag #1: Active Patients

The practice had just 1,100 active patients, well below the 2,000+ sweet spot needed to sustain a full-time doctor. That's like trying to run a restaurant with half the tables full.

Red Flag #2: Cost per Patient

Then we did the math: $900,000 price ÷ 1,100 patients = $818 per patient. That's way above the healthy range of $300–$500. Translation? Lisa would be paying luxury prices for a limited customer base.

Red Flag #3: Collection Potential

In an urban area where each patient typically generates $700/year: 1,100 × $700 = $770,000 in potential annual collections. That's $230,000 short of what the seller claimed in collections the prior year. Something wasn't adding up.

Red Flag #4: Doctor Days

The practice only supported a 3-doctor days per week schedule, with 1,100 active patients. That's not a full-time job; it's a part-time treadmill.

Lisa's heart sank. She realized she wasn't buying a thriving business; she was looking at potential stress, debt, and disappointment. She walked away.

Growth Strategy: Your Reference Guide to Financial Confidence and Practice Evaluation

Metric	What It Means	Target/Benchmark	Why it matters
Active Patients	Patients seen within the last 18 months	◆ 2,000+ for full-time practice	Core indicator of practice strength and patient loyalty
400-Patient Rule	# of active patients per weekly doctor day	◆ 400 = 1 doctor day/week	Ensures schedule, staffing, and revenue capacity
Cost Per Patient	Purchase Price ÷ Active Patients	◆ Aim for $300-$500 Red flag if > $700	Reveals overpaying or poor growth potential
Revenue Potential	Active Patients × Annual Revenue per Patient	◆ According to the ADA: $600 annually estimated patient spend for rural and $700 for urban	Forecasts what the practice could earn under you

Why These Metrics Drive Financial Confidence

These metrics can determine a practice's financial strength and growth potential. By focusing on active patients, capacity, cost per patient, and revenue potential, you can make informed, confident decisions to secure a profitable practice with solid fundamentals.

Active Patients: The Heartbeat of Your Practice

Imagine walking into your dream practice. The chairs are buzzing, the staff is smiling, and patients are raving about their care. What's fueling this magic? Active patients. These are the individuals who have visited your practice at least once in the last 18 months, and they're the lifeblood of your revenue. Without a strong patient base, even the flashiest office is just an empty shell.

Why 18 Months Matters

The 18-month window provides a clear picture of who is loyal and who is just passing through. A single patient who visits multiple times is counted only once. This helps calculate real, sustainable revenue. The more active patients you have, the more predictable your cash flow becomes, and the greater your potential for growth.

The 400-Patient Rule: A Key Metric for Dental Practices

Think of active patients as the driving force behind a dental practice. One of the simplest and most effective methods for assessing a practice's capacity is the 400-patient rule. According to this rule, for every 400 active patients, a practice can reliably schedule one full day of a doctor's services each week.

For instance, in a practice with 800 active patients, there is sufficient demand to support two doctor days each week. Similarly, a practice with 2,000 patients can sustain five doctor days, while 2,800 active patients can keep seven days of dental services running smoothly.

This guideline provides a quick way to evaluate whether a

practice can help you achieve your income goals or if you're investing in a situation characterized by vacant chairs and underutilized staff.

The 400-Patient Rule:
A Quick Overview of Capacity

Active Patients	Doctor Days Supported per Week	Practical Implications
400	1 day	Part-time coverage; limited growth potential.
800	2 days	Part-time coverage; limited growth potential.
1,200	3 days	Steady weekly demand for services.
1,600	4 days	Full clinical schedule begins to form.
2,000	5 days	Full-time doctor with strong utilization.
2,400	6 days	Ready for expansion and growth.
2,800	7 days	Multi-doctor model or extended operating hours.

This table provides a clear framework for understanding how patient volume correlates with doctor availability and practice growth potential.

Key Financials: The Secret Formula for Smart Practice Buys

One of the fastest ways to know if a practice is overpriced? Use this formula: Cost per patient = purchase price ÷ active patients

Metric	Benchmark	Buyer Interpretation
Target Range	$300–$500 per patient	✓ Healthy valuation, strong demand
Caution Zone	$500–$700 per patient	⚠ Requires justification (growth potential, margins, location)
Red Flag	$700+ per patient	⚐ High risk—especially for first-time buyers

Case Study: Same Price, Different Reality

Practice	Location	Purchase Price	Active Patients	Cost per Patient	Verdict
Practice A	Rural	$850,000	2,800	$304	✓ Smart Buy
Practice B	Urban	$850,000	1,200	$708	⚐ Risky

On paper, the two practices look identical in price. In reality, one is a safe, cash-flowing buy. The other is a financial trap.

CEO Insight: According to data published by the American Dental Association in *"The Per-Patient Cost of Dental Care, 2013: A Look Under the Hood,"*) the average annual spending per patient in urban areas was about $685 before 2020. With post-COVID inflation, it's safer to use updated estimates: roughly $600 per patient annually in rural markets and closer to $700 per patient in urban markets. While some buyers may project higher numbers, I prefer to stay conservative with forecasts.

But no matter the location, the formula doesn't lie: if the cost per patient is too high, you'll spend years digging out of the hole.

CEO Story: The Rural Rocket

When Dr. Jamie graduated dental school, most of her classmates sprinted to urban DSOs and sleek metro practices. She went rural and it changed everything.

At Purchase

- Price: $700K

- Active Patients: 3,000

- Cost Per Patient: $233

Her Moves

- Extended hours (two evenings/week)

- Expanded services (same-day crowns + implants)

Two Years Later

- Collections: $2M

- Revenue per Patient: $667

- Net Income: $800K/year

The right numbers turned a small-town buy into a million-dol-lar enterprise.

Dr. Jamie's Takeaway: "I didn't need a better building or a fancier zip code. I just needed to unlock the value already in front of me."

Revenue Potential: The Hidden Upside

Active patients don't just measure the size of a practice, they forecast future revenue. Multiply active patients by annual revenue per patient to see what the practice should be collecting.

Benchmarks

- Rural: Approximately $600 per patient annually

- Urban: Approximately $700 per patient annually

Example

- Urban practice: 2,400 active patients

- 2,400 × $700 per patient annually = $1.68M potential revenue

- Current collections = $1.2M

- Growth Gap: $480,000 waiting to be unlocked

This metric flips the lens from defense (avoiding overpaying) to offense (spotting upside).

Quick Reference: CEO Formulas

Keep these in your pocket. If you can do them on a napkin, you'll never overpay for a practice.

- Active Patients Rule: 400 patients = 1 doctor day per week

- Cost per Patient: Purchase price ÷ active patients (aim for $300–$500)

- Net income as a percentage of collections: 40%+ signals a healthy, bankable practice with margin for growth and stability. Remember to include discretionary add-backs into your net income calculation.

- Practice Value (Ballpark): Net Income × 2–3 (or more if strong growth)

If cost per patient > $700 or net income < 40% of collections, you've spotted a red flag.

Life Lesson: How the Numbers Landed Dr. Sandra the Deal

Dr. Sandra was competing against three other buyers for a suburban practice listed at $1.4M. The office looked average: six ops, outdated chairs, and a seller eager to retire. Most buyers hesitated.

But Sandra ran the metrics:

- Active Patients: 2,500 → strong base, above the 2,000 benchmark.

- Cost Per Patient: $1.4M ÷ 2,500 = $560 → slightly above the sweet spot but manageable.

- Revenue Potential: At $700 per patient (urban average), the practice could generate $1.75M annually, $300K more than current collections.

- 400-Patient Rule: Enough demand to justify bringing on an associate in the next 24 months.

Armed with this, Sandra showed the bank the upside. While competitors saw "overpriced," she saw undervalued potential. She secured financing, closed the deal, and within 18 months grew collections to $1.7M by tightening hygiene recall and adding same-day crowns.

Her words: "The other buyers guessed. I calculated. That's why I won."

Executive Summary

1. **Active patients are the life force of the practice**. Track patients seen in the last 18 months. 2,000+ active patients = a stable, income-generating foundation.

2. **400-Patient Rule** = 1 Doctor Day. Use this metric to gauge scheduling viability and owner income potential.

3. **Cost per patient reveals true value**: $300–$500 = smart buy. Over $700? You're overpaying for risk.

4. **Revenue potential is predictable**. Active Patients × Annual Revenue per Patient shows if the deal can fund your goals.

5. **Net income is non-negotiable**. A healthy practice runs at 40%+ net (with add-backs). Below that, you're buying overhead, not profit.

6. **Let data guide you**. Don't fall in love with the paint color. Fall in love with the patient count.

Action Plan: The Essential Metrics for Practice Valuations

7. Collect real data, not estimates: Gather key metrics from one real practice (yours or a target acquisition): active patients, collections, and net income.

8. Apply the 400-patient rule: How many doctor days would the practice support based on its patient base?

---

9. Benchmark against target: Calculate the cost per patient for a practice you're evaluating. Is it in the $300–$500 range, or does it signal risk?

---

10. Spot the opportunity (or the risk): Estimate the annual revenue potential (Active Patients × Average Revenue per Patient). Determine whether the practice's earning capacity aligns with the growth and financial freedom you're aiming for.

---

11. Build your practice dashboard: Summarize all key metrics, benchmarks, and insights on a single page that gives you an instant snapshot of a practice's financial health and growth potential.

CEO Toolkit

Download the Essential Metrics Cheat Sheet printable PDF—which includes blank fields for your own numbers and quarterly tracking at: *www.TransitionOne.net/DentistToCEO/Toolkit*

Chapter 7:
Building on the Fundamentals –
How to Spot Growth and Upside in a Practice

A Tale of Two Buyers

Dr. Kevin and Dr. Alicia each purchased a million-dollar practice. Same asking price. Same number of ops. On paper, they were buying the same thing. But their futures couldn't have been more different.

Kevin used the metrics from Chapter 6 like a weapon. He saw strong patient flow, efficient overhead, and a cost per patient in the sweet spot. He knew the bank would say yes, the cash flow would fund growth, and within three years, he'd be ready for expansion.

Alicia looked only at the top line. A million dollars in collections sounded safe. She missed the warning signs: overhead creeping past 60%, only four ops, and fewer than 1,500 active patients. Within 18 months, she was trapped, struggling to pay debt service and covering payroll out of her own pocket.

Same price. Different perspectives. Two radically different outcomes.

The Four Levers of Buying Power

When you evaluate a practice, you're not just checking numbers. You're looking for leverage. These four levers can make or break your buying power

1. **Revenue—Top-Line Power**

Revenue shows what the practice can produce under current ownership. But numbers alone don't tell the whole story. Look at the trend: steady, declining, or rising? A flat trend with solid systems may be the best value.

2. **Overhead—The Profit Gatekeeper**

Staff wages, rent, and labs usually consume 55–65 % of collections. Every point you save in overhead is a permanent raise. Find where money leaks—then seal the hole.

3. **Production Mix—The Growth Engine**

A GP who refers out implants, ortho, or clear aligners leaves

10–20% of revenue on the table. Expanding your clinical mix multiplies both income and equity value.

4. Patient Flow—The Lifeline

Track new-patient volume and hygiene recall. Declining flow means value erosion. Consistent flow means predictable income and a stable valuation. Each lever reveals what the practice can control today. But great buyers look beyond the obvious metrics. They search for what others missed.

Life Lesson: The Turnaround—From Flat to Flourishing

When Dr. Aaron purchased Willow Creek Dental, the numbers appeared stable but uninspiring: $1.1 million in collections, five operatories, and hygiene averaging at just 20% of production. The seller called it "maxed out."

But Aaron saw what others didn't—*leverage hiding in plain sight:* thousands of patients and a recall system that was not doing its job.

He added a sixth operatory, hired a second hygienist, and established a basic recall system that reached every inactive patient from the last 18 months. Within a year, the new-patient flow increased by 30%, hygiene accounted for 27% of collections, and revenue surpassed $1.6 million.

The best part? Overhead dropped from 66% to 59% because

fixed costs stayed the same while production increased. That shift raised the practice's valuation by nearly **$700,000** within 18 months.

CEO Insight: You don't need to double production to double value. You just need to make the existing systems produce what they were designed to.

The Compounding Influence of Small Levers

- **+5% hygiene reactivation → +10% production**

- **−3% supply overhead → +$30,000 annual cash flow**

- **+1 new service per year → +$100,000 average revenue lift**

- **+1% improved case acceptance → thousands in retained value**

Translation: Growth isn't about adding more—it comes from tightening the levers that already work.

CEO Story: Ethan vs. Claire

Dr. Ethan and Dr. Claire both had the same goal: to buy their first practice.

Ethan chased numbers. He fell in love with a $1.5M office and assumed "bigger is better." But he never ran the cost per patient, never checked overhead, and never asked how many true active patients the practice had. Within six months, he realized the collections were inflated by discounts and high turnover. The practice looked great on paper, but left him drowning in debt.

Claire chased value. Instead of being dazzled by the top line, she ran the CEO metrics:

- Active patients: 2,650

- Cost per patient: $415

- Net income: 42%

The office was listed at $1.1M, but Claire knew it was underpriced. Why? Because the metrics revealed a solid patient base (well above 2,000 active patients), relatively low cost per patient (within the $300–$500 range), and strong profitability. She bought it, stabilized the staff, and within three years had grown collections to $1.6M, without overextending herself on day one.

Same market. Same opportunity. Two very different outcomes because one chased size, the other chased buying power.

CEO Insight: The Hidden Ceiling in Practice Growth

Every practice has a built-in ceiling. You can hire the best team, refine your schedule, and market like crazy, but if you don't have adequate operatories, eventually you will hit a wall. Chairs are for capacity. Without them, you're trapped in a single-doctor treadmill, no matter how talented you are.

The ownership sweet spot is 5+ operatories.

Active patients are the heartbeat of a practice. Operatories are the lungs. They determine how much capacity you can actually breathe. Too few chairs, and growth becomes impossible. Five or more operatories is a good measure of the health of a practice. The number 5 is the threshold where practices move from survival to scalability.

1. **Revenue Capacity: Chairs = Production**

- 3 or fewer ops: Constant bottlenecks, one-doctor limitation, constant scheduling constraint

- 5+ ops: Hygienists keep flow steady, emergencies don't derail production, and there's room for expansion

Key takeaway: More chairs equal more productive hours in the day

2. **Scalability: Built-in Runway**

- A 2–3 op office may work today, but it boxes you in within 24 months.

- With over 5, you can extend hours, add providers, or launch high-value services like implants and ortho.

Consider operatories as square footage in real estate. Without space, you can't expand.

3. Avoid Costly Remodels Later

- Adding ops later = $50K–$75K per chair, plus permits, downtime, and disruption

- The ability to buy capacity upfront saves you money, time, and headaches.

Advantage: 5+ ops protect your capital and preserve your momentum.

4. Practice Value: What Banks and Buyers See

- Higher appraisal value

- Larger buyer pool when it's time to sell

- More favorable loan approval odds

Key Takeaway: More operatories don't just mean more space for more patients. They also add confidence for you, your lender, and your eventual buyer.

Metrics Are the Language of Capability

Active patients. Cost per patient. Doctor days. Operatories. They're not just numbers—they're levers of control.

Dentists who understand them build momentum and wealth.

Those who don't fall behind and wonder why. As a protentional buyer, do more than comparing practices. This choice will be how you'll live, how you'll lead, and how your family will thrive.

When the paint peels and the "potential" fades, only the math tells the truth. Think like a CEO; be deliberate, data-driven, and disciplined. Because the moment you master your numbers is the moment you take control of your future.

Executive Summary

1. **Think like a CEO**. Compare, don't romanticize. Don't fall in love with aesthetics. Line up the metrics: active patients, doctor days, revenue potential. If the math doesn't map to your goals, it's not the right deal.

2. **Operatories = Opportunity**. Three chairs will stall your growth. Five or more will create capacity for hygiene, emergencies, and eventually an associate. Capacity creates wealth.

3. **Overhead discipline fuels growth**. Overhead at over 60% drains momentum. Lean practices breathe easier and grow faster.

4. **Rural ROI**. Urban offices look flashy, but rural practices build fortunes. Lower overhead, loyal patients, bigger margins. You can retire 10 years earlier in a small town

while your peers grind in the city.

5. **Lisa's story was almost a $900K mistake**. In Chapter 6, Lisa nearly bought a part-time job disguised as a dream. But the numbers told the truth, and she listened. Be like Lisa: run the numbers first, fall in love second.

6. **Metric mastery**. Every number you understand becomes a decision you control. Cost per patient, revenue potential, doctor days . . . these are your foundation. Look to the data as a guide; it will protect you.

Action Plan: Building on the Fundamentals – How to Spot Growth and Upside in a Practice

1. Compare two real practices side by side. Gather active patient counts, operatories, collections, and net income for two different listings. Seeing numbers together clarifies where true value—and risk—really lie. (Worksheet also in the CEO toolkit)

____

____

2. Evaluate the four levers of buying power. Assess each practice for its location economics, patient base stability, operatory capacity, and overhead efficiency. Mark each as a strength, neutral, or weakness. (Worksheet also in the CEO toolkit)

____

____

____

3. Identify the hidden upsides. Look for easy wins
    the seller hasn't captured—unused operatories, low
    marketing spend, outsourced procedures, or weak recall
    systems. Each represents built-in equity waiting to be
    unlocked.

____

____

____

4. Calculate the growth gap. Estimate what the practice
    should be collecting using patient count times the
    average annual revenue per patient. The difference
    between potential and current collections is your
    opportunity window. (Worksheet also in the CEO
    toolkit)

____

____

____

5. Build your value discovery dashboard. Create a simple
    one-page summary of both practices showing red
    flags, upside potential, and deal readiness at a glance.
    This becomes your personal due diligence template.
    (Worksheet also in the CEO toolkit)

____

____

____

CEO Toolkit

Download the Practice Opportunity Assessment Worksheet—a plug-and-play tool that compares metrics, highlights upside, and scores opportunities by fit and risk at: _www.TransitionOne.net/DentistToCEO/Toolkit_

PART IV: FROM RISK TO REWARD—MASTERING THE DEAL

Chapter 8:
Reading the P&L
Like a Detective

Mindset Shift: The P&L speaks clearly when you know how to read it—it highlights where profit is protected and where it's vulnerable.

The Crime Scene

A Profit & Loss statement is like a crime scene. Every line item leaves evidence. Some reflect reality; others mask underlying problems. I've seen sellers hide vacation homes under rent, ghost employees on payroll, even disguise country club dues as marketing. If you don't learn to read a P&L like a detective, you're stepping into a financial trap.

The problem? Most buyers glance at a P&L like it's background noise. They skim the top line (collections), glance at the bottom line (net income), and nod when the broker says, "Looks good." That's like admiring a house while ignoring the broken window and muddy footprints—and still assuming it's safe.

But the truth is that money always leaves a trail. If payroll is bloated, it shows. If the owner is padding his expenses, you'll see it. If the net income looks suspiciously low, there's usually a reason and often an opportunity. The P&L is where the story hides, and only the buyers who know how to read it uncover the real value.

Think of it this way: Tax returns are written to minimize taxes. They're legal camouflage. But the P&L? That's the seller's diary. It records how the practice actually runs day by day, every dollar earned, every dollar spent. Read it right, and you'll get an insight into whether a practice can fund your future.

The Detective's Expense Checklist

Healthy practices tend to reflect a predictable range of expense. If numbers fall outside these ranges, something's off. Don't ignore it—investigate.

Category	Healthy Range (Percent of Collections)	What to Watch For
Rent	4–7%	Above 8% → overpaying
Staff wages & benefits	27–32%	Above 32% → overstaffing or misallocating roles
Clinical supplies	5–7%	Rising costs → poor ordering or waste
Lab fees	6–8%	Cosmetic-heavy or poor pricing structure
Marketing	2–4%	Overspending without ROI
Admin/Utilities/Misc	1–3%	Discretionary or untracked costs

Expenses outside these ranges aren't always bad—they're just signals that the seller is either overspending, hiding perks, or masking inefficiencies.

Quick Test: If you see wages over 32%, clinical supplies over 8%, or rent over 8% start digging—that's where the story hides.

Finding the Hidden Gold: Add-backs

Add-backs are the secret weapon of financial due diligence. They're the adjustments that reveal what a practice really earns once personal or one-time expenses are removed.

Common add-back categories:

1. Owner compensation: Salary, benefits, or bonuses beyond market doctor pay

2. One-time expenses: Legal, consulting, or renovation costs that won't recur

3. Personal expenses: Discretionary items like travel, meals, or family payroll

4. Non-cash expenses: Depreciation and amortization

5. Family/related party costs: Above-market rent or wages for non-working family

CEO Insight: Add-backs are where mediocre deals become great ones.

Understanding the Profit & Loss Flow: From Production to Profit

To uncover hidden value within a practice, it's essential to track the flow of money. The Profit & Loss (P&L) statement provides a clear pathway from production to profit, illustrating how cash enters, exits, and ultimately resides within your business.

1. **Collections (Top-Line Revenue)**: This represents the total income generated from all patient care and procedures before any adjustments. Think of it as "What comes in." ↓

2. **Adjustments & Write-Offs**: This category includes insurance discounts, uncollected balances, and patient credits. It reflects "What disappears before you see it." ↓

3. **Net Collections (Real Revenue)**: This is the actual amount collected, representing your true top line after accounting for write-offs.

4. **Operating Expenses (Overhead)**: These are the recurring costs associated with running your business. Typical benchmarks include:

1. Staff wages and benefits: 28–33%

2. Clinical supplies: 5–7%

3. Lab fees: 6–8%

4. Rent: 4–6%

5. Marketing: 2–4%

6. Office/Admin: 1–3%

Think of this as "Where efficiency thrives—or falters." ↓

5. **Operating Margin**: This is calculated by subtracting overhead from revenue, resulting in profit before owner compensation. Consider it as "How efficient your systems truly are." ↓

6. **Owner Compensation / Add-Backs**: This includes your salary, personal expenses, and one-time costs added back to normalize your income. It serves to illustrate "True earning power." ↓

7. **EBITDA (True Practice Profit)**: This stands for Earnings Before Interest, Taxes, Depreciation, and Amortization, representing your practice's operational profit. Think of it as "What potential buyers or banks evaluate." ↓

8. **Debt Service (Loan Payments)**: This covers the costs associated with loans or financing used to acquire or maintain the business. It reflects "The cost of the deal." ↓

9. **Net Income (Take-Home Profit)**: This is the amount remaining after all expenses, representing your real

spendable cash flow. It signifies "The figure that can transform your life."

By closely monitoring each stage of the P&L flow, you can gain valuable insights into your practice's financial health and uncover opportunities for improvement.

Life Lesson: A Deal that Almost Died

I once worked with a dentist named Raj, a meticulous clinician with a knack for detail. He was set to buy a practice collecting $1 million, priced at $850,000. The seller's tax return showed a net income of $250,000, too low to justify the price. Raj's CPA, a family friend with no dental experience, declared the deal "dead on arrival" and advised walking away. Raj was crushed; he'd already envisioned himself leading the practice.

I asked to see the Profit & Loss statement (P&L). Sure enough, it told a different story. The seller's "rent" was $120,000 annually, paid to a family trust that owned the building, $80,000 above the actual mortgage. The staff payroll included $50,000 for the seller's spouse, who didn't work in the practice. Another $20,000 in "legal fees" covered personal real estate deals. After adjusting these expenses, the true net income was $400,000, or 40% of collections, right in the sweet spot.

I sat Raj down. "Your CPA missed this because he doesn't know dentistry. The P&L shows the real profit. This practice is a gem." Raj pushed back, nervous about challenging his CPA, but I urged him to ask the seller about each expense. The seller confirmed every adjustment, and Raj's bank approved the loan. He bought the practice, kept 90% of the patients, and cleared $350,000 in his first year after loan payments.

Detective's 60-second Scan (What to Flag and Why)

- Staff costs greater than 32%: Often indicates overstaffing, misallocated roles, or pay inflation. Verify schedules of the team, individual productivity, and role clarity.

- Facility costs greater than 8%: Can signal above-market rent or related-party markups. If the seller owns the building, normalize to market rates

- Supplies + Lab costs greater than 14%: May indicate pricing issues, leakage, or case mix anomalies. Check vendor contracts and fee schedules.

- Doctor compensation "at zero" or "very high": Normalize to market associate pay (what you'd pay yourself or a hired doctor) to get true operating profit.

- Net income: Healthy 38–42%. 35–38% = investigate. <35% after normalization = caution; understand the "why."

A P&L always tells a story. The question is: are you reading it like an employee, or like a detective?

The Add-back Equation: Finding True Owner Income

Use this formula to uncover what a practice really earns.

Adjusted Net Income (true cash flow) = Net Income + Owner Compensation + Personal Expenses + One-Time Costs + Excess Rent/Mortgage

Before you memorize the formula, understand the problem it solves.

On paper, many dental practices look underwhelming. The profit seems low. The margins feel too tight. But that's often because owner-operators run personal and strategic expenses through the business—items that lower taxable income but don't reflect the practice's true earning power.

Consider this example:

A practice reports **$180,000 in net income**. At first glance, that feels disappointing. But look closer. The owner pays themselves **$220,000** in compensation, runs **$30,000** of personal expenses through the business, incurred **$20,000** in one-time transition costs, and pays **$25,000** above-market rent to an entity they own.

Suddenly, the story changes. When those items are added back, the practice isn't earning $180,000—it's generating **$475,000 in true cash flow** to the owner. That's why serious buyers don't stop at net income. They adjust it.

Adjusted Net Income (True Owner Cash Flow) = Net Income

- Owner Compensation

- Personal Expenses

- One-Time Costs

- Excess Rent or Mortgage

This adjusted figure is what banks, brokers, and experienced buyers rely on to determine valuation, debt capacity, and risk. It reflects what the practice *produces*, not what the tax return minimizes. Skip this step, and you're not negotiating—you're guessing.

CEO Insight: Tax returns can camouflage true earnings; they are written to minimize taxes, not to show reality.

Executive Summary

---

1. **The P&L is your X-ray**. The Profit & Loss statement reveals where money's coming in, where it's leaking out, and whether this practice will fund your future or bury it in overhead. If you're not reading the P&L, you're flying blind.

2. **Follow the 40% rule**. If unadjusted net is less than <30% and still less than <35% after reasonable normalization and add-backs, walk.

3. **Normalize for reality**. Every seller uses the tax code to reduce profit on paper. Your job is to uncover what's real. The truth is in the adjusted totals.

4. **Add-backs change everything**. Add-backs are your leverage. When calculated correctly, they can turn a mediocre deal into a cash-flow machine.

5. **Trust the P&L, not the tax return**. Tax returns minimize taxes, but they do not show profitability. A P&L generated from real-time software like QuickBooks gives you the clearest picture of practice's financial health.

Action Plan: Reading the P&L Like a Detective

1. Interrogate the evidence. Review the latest 12-month Profit & Loss statement. Highlight any expense categories outside the normal ranges.

---

2. Normalize the story. Add back in owner perks (auto, travel, meals, family payroll) to reveal the practice's true profitability. This gives you a clear baseline of Adjusted Net Income—the number that actually matters to a buyer or bank.

---

3. Follow the money trail. Compare the top five expense categories (staff, rent, lab, supplies, marketing) to recommended industry percentages. Which ones are driving or draining profit?

4. Cross-examine revenue vs. reality. Does production align with collections? A large gap could indicate uncollected AR, heavy write-offs, or billing inefficiencies.

5. Summarize your findings. Build a one-page financial report listing three strengths, three risks, and three follow-up questions for the seller or owner of your existing practice. The goal isn't perfection, it's pattern recognition. (Worksheet also included in the CEO Toolkit)

CEO Toolkit

Download the P&L Detective Worksheet—a fillable dashboard that walks you step-by-step through add-backs, category benchmarks, and key questions to uncover the real profitability of any dental practice at: *www.TransitionOne.net/DentistTo-CEO/Toolkit*

Chapter 9:
Red Flags and
Deal Breakers

Mindset Shift: Numbers show performance; red flags reveal risk. Believe the warnings.

Why Red Flags Matter

Every practice looks good on the surface. A busy waiting room. A glossy brochure. A broker whispering, "It won't be on the market long."

But behind the polish, some practices don't offer opportunities, they become a trap. Keep on the lookout for red flags. The dentists who ignore them are risking their freedom, credibility, and years of their lives cleaning up someone else's mess.

This chapter isn't about spreadsheets. You already know how to measure margins and patient counts. This is about courage: having the discipline to walk away when the warning lights flash.

The 3+ Rule: Your Non-negotiable Framework

When evaluating a practice, count the red flags—not excuses. If you identify three or more, you walk away. No exceptions.

1-2 Red Flags → Negotiate

Isolated issues can often be corrected with pricing, terms, or operational changes.

3+ Red Flags → Walk Away

Multiple issues signal structural risk, not bad luck.

Why This Rule Exists

Patterns don't lie. One problem may be fixable. Two might be manageable with discipline and capital. But three or more indicate a system under stress—and stressed systems punish new owners.

CEO Story: The Three-Alarm Practice

Dr. Evan thought he'd found *the one*.

The office was downtown, beautifully designed, and fully built out with six operatories. The practice collected just over $1.3 million a year, and the asking price was $1.05 million, a number that felt aggressive but justifiable for a flagship location.

At first glance, it looked like a win. Then Evan slowed down and started asking the right questions. When he reviewed the Profit & Loss statement, three warning lights came on immediately.

First, payroll was consuming over 40% of collections. That meant the practice wasn't just busy—it was overextended, with too much labor tied into the schedule to comfortably support debt.

Second, the seller claimed a strong patient base, but "active patients" were defined over 24 months. When Evan standardized the count to an honest 18-month window, the true number dropped to 1,150 patients—far fewer than what a six-operatory office needs to stay full.

Third, rent exceeded 9% of collections and was being paid to a related LLC. When Evan asked whether the rent could be brought down to market, the answer was no.

Each issue on its own might have been manageable. Together, they told a different story. Long-term staff contracts locked in high payroll. The landlord wouldn't adjust rent. Patient demand wasn't deep enough to grow out of the problem.

After running the numbers, Evan realized the truth: after loan payments and taxes, the practice would leave him with less than $180,000 a year—not enough for the lifestyle, flexibility, or growth he wanted. So he did something most buyers struggle to do. He walked away.

The Red Flag Gut-Check: Walk or Work It?

Before you get impressed by the asking price, the equipment list, or a "high collections" headline, run this quick filter. You're not just buying a practice—you're buying the stability underneath it. If the foundation is cracked, the numbers won't save you.

Step 1: Scan for "Walk-Away" Thresholds (60 seconds)

Start here because these are the fastest deal-killers:

- Net Profit Margin (unadjusted) under 30% with no meaningful add-backs = cash flow too thin to sustain ownership.
  Rule: If it's <30% unadjusted, you're not buying income— you're buying stress.

- Payroll over 35% of collections = overhead is structurally bloated.
  Rule: If it's >35%, assume "fixing it" will require painful cuts that risk morale and production.

- Rent over 8% of collections = long-term cash flow drag.
  Rule: If it's >8%, treat it like a permanent tax on your future income.

- Capital upgrades over \$75K needed within 12 months (chairs, sterilization, software, HVAC) = hidden bill due immediately.
  Rule: If upgrades are >\$75K, price must adjust—or walk.

- Two+ consecutive years of declining collections = momentum working against you.
  Rule: You can't "out-hustle" a trend you don't understand.

Step 2: Validate the Patient Base (because this is the engine)

Most practices don't fail from bad dentistry—they fail from insufficient demand.

- Standardize "active patients" to 18 months.
  Bold truth: 24 months often inflates. 12 months can understate. 18 months is the most honest middle.

- If a full-time practice has fewer than 1,000 active patients, the schedule will fight you.
  Bold truth: Empty chairs don't show up on a P&L until it's too late.

- Watch for high turnover: new patients coming in while old patients quietly leave.
  Bold truth: That's not growth—it's a revolving door.

Step 3: Question Anything That Sounds "Convenient"

This is where weak deals hide behind vague explanations.

- Murky add-backs (especially "miscellaneous," "supplies," "repairs," or "owner expenses" without receipts).
  Bold rule: If the seller won't verify it, don't count it.

- Collections inflated by one-time events (employee retention credits, insurance settlements, temporary staffing).
  Bold rule: If it can't repeat, it doesn't belong in valuation.

Step 4: Identify Real Growth Levers (or accept the ceiling)

If there's no obvious path to grow, you're buying a capped asset.

- No room to expand (limited operatories, no hygiene capacity, no scheduling flexibility).

- No systems to create demand (weak marketing, inconsistent reactivation, no referral engine).
  Bold truth: If the practice can't grow without you "working harder," the ceiling is already installed.

Step 5: Make the Decision Using the 3+ Rule

Here's the discipline that protects first-time buyers:

- **1–2 red flags**: Work it. Negotiate terms. Ask for proof. Price the risk.

- **3+ red flags**: Walk away. No exceptions.

Why? Because one problem is fixable. Two may be manageable. Three is a pattern—and patterns don't get cheaper after closing.

Final Line: Red flags don't disappear after closing—they convert into payments.

The Only Question That Matters: Is This Risk Paying You Back?

Not all problems are created equal. Some problems punish you after closing. Others pay you for having the courage to take them on.

The skill isn't avoiding risk. The skill is knowing which risks reward ownership.

Risks That Punish You

Walk away when you see:

- Fixed costs you can't change (rent, contracts, debt)

- Declining demand with no clear explanation

- Payroll locked in above productivity

- Capital needs that must be funded immediately just to survive

These problems don't improve with leadership. They compound.

Risks That Pay You

Lean in when you find:

- Family payroll inflating expenses

- Related-party rent above market

- One-time legal, marketing, or transition costs

- Underutilized hygiene or operatories

- Weak systems hiding strong demand

These aren't red flags. They're pricing errors. And pricing errors are how great deals are made.

CEO Insight: If the risk can be fixed with leadership, systems, or time, it may be an opportunity. If the risk is structural, permanent, or contractual, it's a warning.

CEO Story: The Hazard of Emotional Decision Making

Practice A looked like a dream to Dr. Kelley: perfect location with visibility, $1M+ in collections, friendly and smiling staff. But the math screamed "danger":

- Collections: $1,000,000

- Expenses: $725,000

- Net Profit: $275,000 (27.5%)

- Asking Price: $850,000

Red Flags

- Payroll at 45%

- Advertising at 5% with no ROI

- $60K "miscellaneous"

After debt service, cash flow was too minimal to cover loans and salary. The buyer ignored the alarms and bought anyway. Within a year, she was broke.

The Turn: Not Every "Bad" Deal Is Bad

Here's where most dentists miss the big picture: sometimes the ugliest P&L hides the best opportunity.

A messy P&L doesn't always signal danger—it often signals disorganization. And disorganization can be bought at a discount. The key is learning to normalize the numbers—to strip away the noise and see what the practice should earn under competent ownership.

- Maybe staff wages look high because two family members are on payroll.

- Maybe rent seems inflated because the seller owns the building and pays himself above market.

- Maybe "marketing" exploded last year because the office rebranded, and that cost won't repeat.

Each of those adjustments—called add-backs—reshapes the picture of profitability. Once you recast the P&L through that lens, you stop chasing "perfect" practices and start recognizing undervalued ones.

Practice B (How a "Thin" Deal Became Bankable)

Practice B appeared to be a risky bet at first glance:

- Collections: $1,000,000 (6 ops)

- Reported Expenses: $725,000

- Reported Net Profit: $275,000 (27.5%)

- Asking Price: $850,000 (85% of collections)

With margins far below the 40% benchmark, most buyers would've walked.

But here's where financial fluency pays off. Instead of taking the numbers at face value, we normalized expenses and uncovered buried profit.

The Add-Backs that Changed Everything

- **Rent**: $125K reported → should be $50K. Seller was paying $75K above market rent to spouse's LLC. (+75K)

- **Staff Wages**: $360K reported → included $60K salary to spouse. (+60K)

- **Miscellaneous**: $100K reported → included $15K unrelated legal fees. (+15K)

Normalized Net Profit: $425,000 (42.5%)

Why the New Math Works

What looked like only a 27% net income practice was really a 42% net income performer hiding behind poor accounting. Once we stripped out inflated rent, family payroll, and non-practice expenses, the deal went from risky to bankable. At $850 K, the buyer was effectively purchasing a $1M-collection office with owner income exceeding $400 K—a 2-to-1 return on investment from day one.

Life Lesson: The Hidden-Gold Turnaround

Dr. Lila reviewed a practice with $950K in collections. Reported net income: 29%. On the surface: a pass. She scanned for signals: supplies and lab fees at 16% (too high), marketing at 1% (underinvested), and $48K "miscellaneous."

Due diligence showed legacy lab pricing and expired vendor discounts. Marketing was basically zero. "Miscellaneous" hid a one-time IT conversion and non-operational legal bill. After normalizing: net was at 38.5%.

Lila negotiated a price hold, secured vendor resets, and budgeted $1,500/month in targeted marketing. Six months post-close, collections were up 11%, with net holding above 39%.

Takeaway: Not all "bad" P&Ls are a warning to walk away; normalized truth beats first glance.

The Hidden Gold Checklist: Identifying Opportunities Others Overlook

Recognizing red flags can guide you, but uncovering hidden potential is what truly enriches your practice. Often, mismanagement or outdated profit categories conceal valuable opportunities just waiting to be discovered.

- Rent Adjustments by Family LLCs: When family LLCs increase rent, they often bring it down to market levels during a sale, revealing hidden profits.

- Removing Unproductive Roles: If a spouse or relative is employed but not contributing, consider removing that position.

- One-off Legal/Marketing Expenses: These should be added back into your financial analysis.

Threshold: If your adjusted net income increases by 8–12% after these add-backs, you've struck gold.

Untapped Patient Base Potential

- A steady, active patient base of 2,000+ with hygiene revenue contributing less than 20% of total income indicates significant upside potential.

- Ideally, hygiene revenue should represent 25–30% of total practice income. Anything lower often signals a weak recall system, which can be quickly remedied.

Hygiene visits provide consistent income and support restorative work by identifying new treatment needs.

Case Study: Dr. Elena revitalized her practice by re-engaging lost patients, resulting in a 10% increase in collections over six months without acquiring new patients.

Underutilized Operatories

- If you have 5 or more operatories but only 3 are actively in use, there's a growth opportunity without the need for construction.

Threshold: Each unused operatory can represent $150K–$250K in potential annual production.

Owner's Lifestyle Expenses

- Expenses such as country club dues, personal vehicles, and "miscellaneous perks" integrated into the P&L are often unnecessary add-ons.

Threshold: If lifestyle expenses exceed $20K, you have additional margin that can significantly increase your profit at the time of sale.

Strong Patient Loyalty with Minimal Marketing

- A practice with little to no advertising budget can still show healthy growth potential. This suggests that with smarter marketing strategies, you can maximize your growth.

Case Study: Dr. James acquired a practice with no marketing budget. By investing $1,500/month in targeted advertising, he achieved a 30% increase in new patients in his first year.

By diligently analyzing these areas, you can uncover hidden gold that may significantly enhance your practice's value and profitability.

CEO Insight: This set of metrics helps you determine the financial health of a practice, and allows you to invest in a sustainable business with healthy cash flow and loan viability. With an emphasis on these benchmarks, you can be confident about making data-led decisions and be confident that your way to successful practice ownership will follow.

Executive Summary

1. **Numbers don't just reveal value, they reveal danger**. A bad deal doesn't always look bad on the surface. Red flags like inflated payroll, weak margins, and zero add-backs can be alarms. Learn to read them. Trust them. Act on them.

2. **Low net income with no add-backs, walk away**. You can't rescue a practice that's bleeding cash with no margin for growth. Don't let optimism override the math.

3. **Overhead lies in the details**. Line-by-line expenses expose the truth. Watch for rent to family LLCs, bloated payroll, and unexplained costs. Ask the uncomfortable questions.

4. **Not all practices can be fixed**. Some practices are structurally flawed. If you see high fixed overhead and weak patient flow, walk away.

5. **Red flags aren't obstacles, they're filters**. They speed up clarity, save time, and protect your future. When the right deal appears, the numbers, not your emotions, will confirm it.

Action Plan: Red Flags and Deal Breakers

1. Run Your Red-Flag Scan. Review the last three practices you've evaluated. For each, list every red flag you spotted.

   ____

   ____

   ____

2. Score the severity. Rank each red flag as Low, Moderate, or Critical based on impact to cash flow and patient retention. Critical issues demand immediate clarification or exit.

   ____

   ____

   ____

3. Dig one layer deeper. For each flagged item, write a follow-up question you'll ask the seller, CPA, or broker. Red flags aren't always deal-killers, but they're always conversation starters.

   ____

   ____

   ____

4. Create a **simple one-page snapshot** that lists every red flag you've identified, how serious it really is, and what you're going to do about it—**fix it, clarify it, or walk away.**

____

____

____

CEO Toolkit

Uncover the story behind the numbers—and the red flags hiding in the deal. Download the full worksheet and scoring dashboard at: *www.TransitionOne.net/DentistToCEO/Toolkit*

Chapter 10:
Smart Financing
Without the Stress

Same Practice. Different Future.

Dr. Maya and Dr. Jordan each bought nearly identical practices:

- $1.2M in collections

- Strong hygiene programs

- Loyal, stable patient bases

- Comparable teams and equipment

- Same market. Same dentistry.

On paper, these deals looked the same. They weren't. The difference came down to financing.

Dr. Maya: The 7.5% Loan

Dr. Maya accepted a higher interest rate, assuming she'd "grow into it."

Here's what actually happened:

- Monthly loan payment was nearly $2,000 higher than expected

- No room for staff raises

- Marketing budget slashed just to stay afloat

- Equipment upgrades postponed year after year

By Year 3:

- Collections were still stuck at $1.2M

- Cash flow felt tight every month

- Stress became the constant companion of ownership

She didn't fail as a dentist. She was boxed in by her debt.

Dr. Jordan: The 5% Loan

Dr. Jordan secured better terms—and that changed everything.

- Lower monthly payments created immediate cash-flow breathing room

- Early staff raises improved morale and retention

- Consistent investment in marketing drove new-patient growth

- Equipment upgrades expanded case acceptance and efficiency

By Year 3:

- Collections had grown to $1.6M+

- The practice felt stable, confident, and scalable

Same practice. Different trajectory.

Financial Reality Check #4: Understanding Rate, Term and Total Interest Cost

Let's break down what a difference in loan rates can really mean for your finances over the life of a typical $1 million practice loan. Here's a look at three scenarios:

Loan Scenario	Rate	Term	Monthly Payment	Total Interest Paid	Total Cost of Loan
Scenario A: "Great Rate"	6.0%	10 years	$11,100	$332,000	$1.33 Million
Scenario B: "Long Term"	6.0%	15 years	$8,440	$519,000	$1.52 Million
Scenario C: "Cheaper Rate, Same Term"	5.5%	10 years	$10,850	$302,000	$1.30 Million

(This example is based on a $1 million practice loan.)

CEO Insight: The distinction between a good rate and a great rate is more than just a few percentage points; it can translate to years of financial progress. For instance, over the life of a 10-year, $1 million loan, even a half-point difference in interest can lead to an extra $150,000 to $200,000 spent on interest. That's money that could have been reinvested into your practice to fuel growth.

In the end, smart financing doesn't just save you money—it can also provide you with greater financial freedom. The same practice can lead to very different futures depending on your financing choices.

Pro Tip: On a $1.0M loan amortized over 10 years, expect monthly payments to increase by roughly $500 per month for every 1.0% increase in the interest rate.

The 5-Step CEO Financing Playbook

Step 1. Know the Cost of Capital

Not all loans are created equal. A 7.5% interest rate can turn your dream practice into a cash drain. At 5%, the same deal fuels growth. That 2.5% difference? It's hundreds of thousands of dollars over the life of a loan.

CEO Insight: Don't just ask "Can I get approved?" Instead ask: "What will this loan cost me in freedom over 10 years?"

The 3Rs of Smart Financing:

- **Rate:** Compare the total cost of funds—not just the APR.

- **Relationship:** Work with a lender who understands dental cash flow cycles.

- **Restrictions:** Identify covenants and hidden clauses that limit flexibility.

If any one of the three feels off, your deal will also feel off.

Step 2. Understand the Bank's Playbook

Banks don't care how good your crown margins look. They care about cash flow and whether you can pay them back. Here's what underwriters look for:

- Adjusted net income: Just like you, banks normalize expenses. Add-backs directly impact how much income they see available to pay the loan.

- Personal credit and history: Your production record and financial habits speak louder than your résumé.

- Banking relationship: Some lenders require you to move your business banking to them. Make sure you're comfortable with their rates, services, and long-term partnership.

- Liquidity: Banks want to see that you have a financial cushion—cash reserves that prove you can handle short-term surprises once you own the practice. Think of it as your *rainy-day fund* for payroll, repairs, or a slow month. Most lenders expect liquidity equal to **7–10% of the total loan amount.**

How many banks should you call? Always shop at least two lenders and collect written term sheets. Comparing rates, terms, and conditions arms you with leverage and peace of mind.

Translation: Banks aren't betting on your dentistry. They're betting on your ability to think and act like a CEO.

Step 3. Negotiate Financing Like a CEO

You don't have to take the first loan offer. Ask better questions:

- "What's the rate, and is it fixed or variable?"

- "What's the prepayment penalty?" (Some banks lock you in for 5–10 years.)

- "Will you finance working capital?" (Cash buffer for payroll, marketing, upgrades.)

- "What covenants are tied to this loan?" (Hidden clauses can choke flexibility.)

Managing Cash Flow with a Working Capital Line of Credit

Dental practices usually carry accounts receivable (A/R) of 30–45 days, depending on mix of payers and billing efficiency. Insurance-heavy practices often see this grow to 45–60 days with claim processing, denials, and resubmissions. Longer A/R cycles mean the practice delivers care weeks before receiving payment—resulting in temporary cash gaps even when the business is profitable on paper.

A working capital line of credit (LOC) is a flexible financing instrument that helps bridge those gaps. It enables a practice to borrow funds to pay short-term expenses—like payroll, lab fees, or supplies—as needed while waiting for insurance reimbursements or patient payments. Unlike a term loan, you only pay interest on the amount drawn, and funds can be repaid and reused as cash flow normalizes, operating much like a large credit card for your business.

Working capital LOCs can work for even practices with healthy cash reserves because they:

- Preserve liquidity (keeps your cash in savings or investment accounts earning interest while the LOC covers short-term needs),

- Builds business credit (regular, responsible use—borrowing and repaying on time—strengthens your credit profile and improves future loan terms),

- Adds flexibility and supports growth (a safety net for emergency spending, strategic investment in marketing, hiring, or equipment without draining reserves).

Step 4. Play Offense with Leverage

Financing isn't just about surviving debt—it's about using the debt wisely to support the growth of your business.

- Finance wisely, and your patients fund the loan while you build equity.

- Refinance strategically, and you free up cash for expansion.

- Align loan terms with practice growth, not just "getting approved."

CEO Story: I worked with a buyer who almost passed up a practice because the payment looked high. But once we normalized expenses, we saw $320K in real take-home after debt service. The bank said yes. Today, he's debt-free and owns two practices.

Step 5. Keep Psychology in Play

Sellers are people first. Many push for "all cash at closing" because it feels safe, not because it's the smartest structure. As a buyer, you can often win the deal by offering creative options.

- **Seller note**: A portion of the price is financed directly by the seller, and paid back over time with interest.

- **Holdback**: A small amount of the purchase price is withheld until certain conditions are met (e.g., patient retention or transition support).

- **Staged payouts**: Payments spread out over several months or years, often tied to performance milestones.

These structures can often bridge gaps in the purchase price, reduce your upfront burden, and reassure sellers while protecting you.

CEO Insight: The right bank will be a long-term partner. Look for responsiveness and transparency about timelines from application to funding. Some banks can approve and fund a term loan within weeks, while others may take months. Underwriting standards vary widely, so prioritize institutions known for efficient communication, clear documentation, and experience working with dental practices.

Why Smart Financing Wins

Smart financing does more than just get you loan approval; it sets the stage for how debt will impact your financial future. From the moment you take on that debt, it can either become a valuable asset or a burdensome liability.

When done right, smart financing can offer you:

- Lower Monthly Pressure: Say goodbye to constant stress and hello to manageable payments.

- Stronger Cash Flow: Shift from survival-mode budgeting to thriving with your finances.

- Negotiating Power: Step into discussions with confidence, knowing you're not in a desperate situation.

- Freedom to Reinvest: Focus on growing your business through investments in people, marketing, and systems, rather than just scraping by to cover expenses.

The Bottom Line

Debt itself isn't inherently bad; the issue lies in misaligned debt. When your debt aligns with your practice's actual cash flow, it can enhance your decision-making. Conversely, misaligned debt can limit your options and create unnecessary pressure.

One approach opens doors and creates possibilities, while the other can stifle growth. Remember, it's not the dentistry that holds you back—it's the pressure of mismanaged finances.

CEO Insight: Financing can become the backbone of your success. A bad loan can choke your dream, but a smart one sets you free. Take the time to compare lenders, negotiate terms, and lean on experts.

Executive Summary

1. **Financing isn't the enemy, but bad terms are**. With the right lender and structure, financing becomes a step to ownership, not a trap.

2. **Know your numbers before you borrow**. Understand net income, patient count, and cost per patient before you ever talk to a lender.

3. **Choose dental-specific lenders**. Work with banks that understand dental practices, and avoid balloon payments or high-interest pitfalls.

4. **Build a strong application**. A solid business plan, strong credit, and mastery of practice metrics show lenders you're ready to lead.

5. **Match loan terms to your goals**. Ensure monthly payments align with the practice's cash flow to protect your growth runway.

Action Plan: Smart Financing Without the Stress

1. Compare lenders side by side. Gather at least two written loan proposals. List key details: rate, term length, required equity injection, and working capital allowance.

2. Calculate true loan cost. Determine the total interest paid over the life of each loan. Multiply the monthly payment by the number of payments, subtract the loan amount, and you'll see whether a lower rate is actually saving money or just stretching the cost out longer.

____

____

____

3. Read the fine print. Flag any clauses that limit flexibility, such as prepayment penalties, mandatory banking relationships, or restrictive covenants. Every loan should protect your upside—not trap your growth.

____

____

____

4. Build your lender comparison sheet. Summarize all proposals on one page: lender, total cost, hidden fees, and qualitative notes (responsiveness, expertise, flexibility). Then, select your financial partner—not just your lender. (Worksheet also included in the CEO Toolkit)

____

____

____

CEO Toolkit

Download the Dental Loan Comparison Dashboard, a plug-and-play spreadsheet that calculates total loan cost and repayment scenarios so you can choose the financing partner that aligns with your long-term ownership goals at: _www.TransitionOne.net/DentistToCEO/Toolkit_

PART V:
WINNING HEARTS, NOT JUST NUMBERS

Chapter 11:
Protecting the Asset You Can't Replace:
Seller Goodwill

Mindset Shift: Banks don't fund goodwill. Brokers can't appraise it. But goodwill is the real purchase price. Numbers might buy you a practice, but goodwill is what keeps it alive.

The Dinner that Closed the Deal

Three offers sat on Dr. Kevin's desk. One was $75,000 higher than the rest. On paper, it was the obvious choice. But when Kevin picked up his pen, he paused. He couldn't shake the memory of one simple dinner conversation.

Dr. Todd, a young buyer, had invited Dr. Kevin and his wife, Katherine, out after their first meeting. No contracts. No negotiations. Just pasta, wine, and stories. Todd asked about the practice's history, the team's journey, even Kevin's retirement dreams. He listened more than he talked.

Later that night, Katherine leaned over and said, "That young man didn't feel like a buyer. He felt like family."

The next day, Kevin turned down the higher bid and told his broker, "I'm going with the one who'll honor what I built."

Six months after closing, Todd hadn't lost a single staff member. Patient retention was 97%. Kevin still stopped by with referrals and coffee.

Todd didn't win on price. He won on goodwill.

The Goodwill Equation – Defined

Think of goodwill as the invisible infrastructure of a dental practice. It's what makes the numbers repeatable after ownership changes hands.

Goodwill = Seller Trust + Patient Loyalty + Staff Stability

Seller Trust

This is the confidence the seller places in you as the next owner. It shows up through a smooth transition, honest disclosures, patient introductions, and the seller's willingness to support continuity. When seller trust is strong, patients and staff feel reassured rather than abandoned.

Patient Loyalty

This reflects how attached patients are to the practice, not just the dentist. Loyal patients keep appointments, accept treatment, and stay through ownership changes. Without patient loyalty, collections dip the moment the seller steps away.

Staff Stability

This is the strength and continuity of the team that runs the daily operation. Stable staff preserve systems, culture, and patient experience. High turnover after a sale is one of the fastest ways to destroy goodwill.

Why It Matters

If even one of these elements is weak, goodwill erodes—and so does value. But when all three are strong, you're not just buying equipment and charts—you're inheriting a self-sustaining operation built to perform from day one.

Why Likability Is Your Secret Weapon

Picture this: You're sitting across from a seller who's spent decades building their practice. This business is their pride, their community, their life's work. They're not going to hand it over to just anyone with a checkbook.

They want to give it to someone they like. Someone they trust. Someone who will carry on their legacy.

Don't just charm or flatter the buyer, win them over by showing them respect. Show up as a genuine partner who honors what they've built.

Why it matters: How much they like you can be a deal-closer. It can mean the seller even lowers their price to work with you. A positive interpersonal relationship keeps goodwill intact, ensuring patients and staff stay after the sale.

New Buyers Growth Strategy: Essential Tips Before Signing the Contract

Step 1: Assess Key Metrics Before Entering Negotiations

To ensure your time—and the seller's—is well spent, verify these five essential criteria. These benchmarks will help you distinguish between scalable opportunities and potential pitfalls.

- **Operatories: 5+**

    A practice should have at least five operatories to provide operational flexibility. This capacity allows you to increase hygiene days, enhance doctor productivity, or introduce new services without incurring immediate real estate or construction expenses. Fewer operatories mean that growth will necessitate additional capital before generating any revenue.

- **Active Patients: 2,000+**

    A robust active patient base is crucial for maintaining consistent demand and fully booked schedules. Insufficient patient numbers can lead to empty chairs, underutilized staff, and unpredictable income, undermining even the most well-managed practice.

- **Net Income: 40%+ of Collections**

  This margin is essential for ensuring adequate cash flow to service debt, offer competitive salaries, and reinvest in the practice. Margins below this threshold leave little room for unexpected challenges, an inevitability in the field of dentistry.

- **Cost per Patient: < $500**

  This metric can indicate whether the asking price is justified by actual demand. A lower cost per patient suggests fair market value and manageable risk. Conversely, higher figures may require aggressive production efforts just to break even.

- **Seller Support: 3–6 Months**

  A smooth transition is vital. Sufficient seller involvement during this period helps stabilize patient retention, reassures staff, and preserves goodwill. Limited or hurried transitions can lead to patient attrition and team turnover both costly complications in the initial year.

Pro Tip: If a practice fails to meet these criteria, it may not be a viable opportunity—it could be a distraction instead. Protect

both your time and the seller's by confirming these metrics before entering discussions.

Step 2. The Meet and Greet: Build Trust, Not Deals

Your first meeting is not about signing a contract, it's about making a human connection.

- Bring your human side: If possible, include your spouse or partner. Sellers connect with families, not résumés.

- Focus on their story: Ask questions like "What made this practice special to you?"

- Read the room: Don't nitpick if you see old chairs or equipment. Pay close attention to the practice's overall culture, longevity of staff, and quality of patients.

Why it matters: This is your chance to show you're not just buying a practice, you're honoring their reputation.

Step 3. Build a Bridge of Trust

Approach the seller as a transition partner—not just a transaction.

- Share your "why":
  "What drew me to this practice is _____. Here's what I hope to build—does that align with what you want for the practice?"

- Learn their vision:
  "When you picture the future of this practice after you step away, what matters most to you?"

- Acknowledge their work:
  "What are you most proud of in the practice you've built here?"

- Ask smart, early questions:
  "How long has the core team been together?"
  "What's the landlord relationship been like?"
  "Have you seen changes in patient volume or retention recently?"

Pro Tip: Avoid price talk at this stage. Connection first. Numbers later.

Step 4. Negotiate with Respect, Not Aggression

Your objective isn't just to buy a practice—it's to inherit the goodwill that makes it work.

- Anchor price to metrics:
  "Based on patient count, margins, and cost per patient, how does the current price reflect those fundamentals?"

- Clarify transition support:
  "Would you be open to a 3–6 month transition period and a jointly signed patient letter to ensure continuity and confidence?"

- Confirm fair noncompete terms:
  "Can we align on a noncompete that protects the practice without restricting future opportunities—typically 10 miles in urban areas or 15–20 miles in rural markets?"

- Set a professional diligence window:
  "To do this right, can we agree on a 60–90 day due diligence period with refundable earnest money tied to verification of the numbers?"

 **Do Ask:**

"How can we make this transition smooth for patients and staff?"

Don't Do:

Lowball offers framed as "starting points." Offering $600K on a $900K practice damages trust instantly—and trust is part of what you're buying

Why Respect Wins

Fair, metric-based negotiation preserves goodwill—the very asset that keeps patients loyal and staff committed after the handoff. Lose that, and even a "great price" becomes expensive.

Understanding Seller Psychology

Your seller will probably have a lot of emotions about selling their business. Learn to read between the lines to understand their feelings.

"I want to ensure my legacy continues."

- **Translation:** The seller struggles with life after dentistry and may fear losing their identity.

- **Resolution:** Acknowledge their legacy. Position yourself, the buyer, as a steward, not a disruptor. Offer to keep the seller's name on signage for a period, retain key traditions, or highlight their role in mentoring the next generation.

"It's not about the money."

- **Translation:** It's about the money—this could be a sign of their financial anxiety.

- **Resolution:** Build trust through transparency. Show that your financing is solid, your production plan is realistic, and that the seller's earn-out or note is secure. Give them confidence that the business they built is in financially capable hands.

"I want to make sure the team is taken care of."

- **Translation:** There may be hidden staff or morale issues, and they may feel guilty about abandoning their staff.

- **Resolution:** Lead with empathy. Stress continuity of culture as a priority. Provide staff retention bonuses, maintain benefits, and communicate early with the team to set a foundation of stability under new ownership.

"I need to stay involved post-sale."

- **Translation:** The seller has a hard time letting go, and this is a sign they may have control issues.

- **Resolution:** Define clear but respectful boundaries. Offer a short-term transition or associate agreement that gives them purpose and structure while ensuring leadership fully transitions to you.

CEO Insight: Numbers close deals. But psychology makes or breaks transitions. The best CEOs manage both—addressing the seller's fears without surrendering leverage. When you resolve emotions with empathy and facts, you earn trust, which is what truly closes the deal.

The Goodwill Equation: How Trust Becomes Tangible Value

Component	What It Represents	Why It Matters
Seller Trust	Confidence that the buyer will prioritize the well-being of patients, staff, and the practice's legacy.	Building trust reduces friction in negotiations, strengthens terms, and can save you significant amounts—often six figures—during the process.
Staff Loyalty	Stability within the team, continuity of the practice's culture, and familiarity for patients.	Keeping staff on board translates to consistent production, which is crucial for a successful transition.
Patient Retention	The trust and confidence the community has in the practice, ensuring continuity of care after the sale.	Retaining patients drives recurring revenue and helps maintain the value of your reputation.
Systems & Reputation	The reliability of processes, strong referral networks, and a solid local presence.	These elements turn the concept of goodwill into predictable profit, making the practice more appealing.

In essence, Goodwill = Trust × Transferability. A seamless transition can enhance the value of a practice even more than a mere 5% increase in price—because having a motivated seller, a loyal team, and dedicated patients provides invaluable leverage.

CEO Story: The Power of Trust

Dr. Sarah discovered a 5-operatory practice with $1 million in collections, 2,500 active patients, $410,000 net income, and a $900,000 price tag.

Before she discussed price, Sarah invested time to understand the business. She visited the practice, met with the team, and even invited the seller and his spouse to dinner. When it came time to make an offer, she proposed $850,000, explaining that she would need funds for new computers and software. She also asked for a four-month transition period and a patient letter of introduction.

The seller accepted, even adding six months of personal support and a glowing patient endorsement. The results? Sarah retained 95% of patients and grew collections to $1.4 million within two years.

Her secret? She won the seller's trust before ever talking about price.

Negotiation Dos and Don'ts

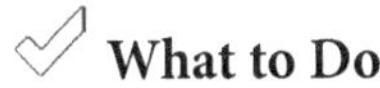 **What to Do:**

- **Use inclusive language:** Instead of framing requests in a way that feels confrontational, try saying, "How can we structure this to meet both our goals?" This kind of collaborative language helps build trust and keeps the conversation focused on solutions.

- **Ask open-ended questions:** Encourage dialogue by asking, "How can we make this transition as smooth as possible for both patients and staff?" This invites more thoughtful responses and fosters a collaborative atmosphere.

- **Show respect for the seller›s hard work:** Remember that the practice represents years of effort and dedication. Valuing that goodwill can often be more beneficial than simply negotiating for a lower price.

- **Protect your interests:** Negotiate terms that ensure a smooth transition, such as 60–90 days for due diligence, 3–6 months of transition support, and a reasonable noncompete clause.

- **Aim for mutual success:** Remember that in addition to acquiring a practice, you're also gaining trust. A successful negotiation is one where both parties feel like winners.

- **Be clear and flexible:** While it's important to be open to adjustments in timing or transitions, clarity is key. Make sure that every verbal agreement is documented in writing before you sign the Letter of Intent (LOI) or purchase agreement.

What Not to Do:

- **Avoid starting with a lowball offer:** This approach can damage goodwill right from the start and may set a negative tone for the negotiation.

- **Don't ignore red flags in the Profit and Loss statement:** Be cautious about overinflated payroll figures, a low active patient count, or poor profit margins. These could indicate deeper issues.

- **Don't get bogged down in minor details:** Focus on the essentials rather than getting stuck on furniture, carpet, paint, or other cosmetic concerns.

- **Keep your focus on the bigger picture:** Remember that the terms of the deal are just as important as the price itself.

- **Don't let emotions cloud your judgment:** While it's important to respect the seller's story, make sure to rely on the numbers and facts when making decisions.

CEO Insight: How you negotiate sets the stage for your future ownership. Be assertive yet fair, and keep in mind that the seller is not just transferring a practice to you—they are entrusting you with their life's work.

Bridge to Chapter 12: Goodwill with the seller gets you to the closing table. But goodwill doesn't end there, it has to transfer into your professional life as a business owner. The real test begins the day you hang your name on the door: will patients stay, will staff follow, will the community embrace you? That's where the next chapter takes us.

Executive Summary

1. **Likeability closes deals.** Sellers are handing off decades of relationships, not just a ledger. Trust and rapport often matter more than numbers.

2. **Listen first, lead later**. Use your first meeting to understand the seller's story, values, and relationships before talking price.

3. **Bring the human side**. Include your spouse or partner, and share your vision. People buy into people before they buy into terms.

4. **Negotiate with respect**. Skip the lowball offers. Focus on value, transparency, and win-win terms that preserve goodwill.

5. **Lock in transition support**. Require a seller's patient letter, personal endorsement, and 3–6 months of post-sale support to protect retention.

6. **Seller goodwill sets the stage**. How you treat the seller sets the tone for patients and staff.

Action Plan: Protecting the Asset You Can't Replace: Seller Goodwill

1. Identify your non-negotiables for preserving goodwill — Define in writing what you must have for the deal to make sense—financing terms, transition support, working capital, or staff retention. Clear boundaries create confident negotiations.

2. Keeping goodwill within the guardrails—Before signing the LOI or purchase agreement, every verbal promise needs to be reflected in writing. Go to the legal templates on our website and try drafting an agreement tailored to your practice and terms.

CEO Toolkit

Download the Goodwill Protection & Transition Playbook—which includes a full timeline, editable staff meeting agenda, and goodwill clause templates at: _www.TransitionOne.net/DentistToCEO/Toolkit_

Chapter 12:
Leading Like a CEO – Preserving Goodwill with Patients, Staff, and Community

Mindset Shift: When you buy a business, you also inherit its reputation. Sellers, staff, and patients aren't looking for a buyer. They're hoping for a worthy successor.

When goodwill transfers, everything works.

When Dr. Chester sold his practice at 68, the numbers made sense: $1.2M in collections, healthy margins, fair price. But what sealed his legacy wasn't just good financing; it was a simple gesture made at a staff meeting.

He shook the hand of his young buyer, turned to his staff, and said, "This is my dentist now. You can trust her the way you trusted me."

That one sentence carried more weight than $10,000 in marketing. Staff and patient retention was near 100%. The buyer inherited decades of credibility on day one.

Contrast that with another buyer's experience. The seller, feeling disrespected, left bitterly without informing his patients or making staff introductions. Within twelve months, a third of the patient base was gone. The buyer didn't lose money because of the numbers. He lost it because goodwill walked out the door.

That's the lesson: Goodwill has no value unless it transfers.

The Four Bridges of Goodwill

If you want patients to stay, staff to commit, and the community to welcome you, you have to build bridges. As we outlined in the previous chapter, **Step One is creating a bridge with the seller.**

1. Bridge with the Seller

- How to build it: Approach the seller with humility and respect. Ask about their proudest moments. Acknowledge what they've built.

- Why it works: When a seller endorses you, their credibility becomes yours. That handshake can be worth more than any contract clause.

CEO Insight: A seller's blessing in the lobby is worth more than a billboard on the highway.

Once the seller bridge is in place, the next relationship that determines whether the practice stabilizes or fractures is the staff.

2.   Bridge with the Staff

- Build It: Meet them early in the process. Listen before you talk. Share your vision, but respect their routines.

- Why it works: Staff are the guardians of culture. If they believe in you, patients will too.

Pro Tip: Win the team, and you'll keep the patients. Lose the team, and you'll lose both.

Financial Reality Check #5 – The Cost of Staff Turnover Based on $1,000,000 in Annual Collections

Let's face it: a revolving door of employees is not a sustainable way to grow your practice. It's important to understand the real financial impact of staff turnover on your bottom line. Here's a breakdown of what losing just one employee can cost you:

Position	Average Annual Salary	Replacement & Retraining Cost (2–3 × Salary)	10% Lost Production Efficiency (3 Months)	Total Annual Financial Impact per Departure
Dental Assistant	$45,000	$90,000	$25,000	$115,000
Hygienist	$80,000	$160,000	$25,000	$185,000
Office Manager	$70,000	$140,000	$25,000	$165,000

How the Lost Production Numbers Were Derived (Role by Role)

Dental Assistant – 10% disruption to revenue over a 3-month period

Assistants don't produce directly but when they're missing or inexperienced, doctors slow down, chair turnover drops and small inefficiencies compound across the schedule.

Hygienist – 10% disruption to revenue over a 3-month period

When a hygienist leaves, hygiene chairs sit empty, recall slips, and preventative visits are often lost, sometimes permanently. This is one of the most immediate and visible hits to production. Missed hygiene today often means lost patients tomorrow.

Office Manager – 10% disruption to revenue over a 3-month period

When an office manager turns over, scheduling errors occur, A/R is delayed, reimbursements are disrupted and communication breakdowns create operational inefficiencies.

Why These Numbers Are Conservative

What is not included:

- Patient attrition from missed hygiene

- Decline in case acceptance

- Burnout-driven secondary turnover

- Reputation or review damage

- Owner distraction during transition

Those costs are real but harder to quantify so they're excluded. This makes these figures a floor, not a ceiling.

3. **Bridge with the Patients**

How to Build This Connection: Start by co-signing a transition letter with the outgoing dentist. Make sure to display clear signage about the change. Update your website and social media channels to reflect your new role. Most importantly, when you're face-to-face with your patients, look them in the eye and reassure them by saying, "You're in good hands."

Why It Works: Remember, patients don't typically leave their dentists; they leave when they start feeling uncertain. Open and clear communication helps to keep them grounded and reassured.

Pro Tip: Don't delay introductions. Rumors fill the silence faster than facts.

4. Bridge with the Community

How to Build This Connection: Get involved in your community by attending local events, supporting a Little League team, or joining service clubs.

Why It Works: By becoming an active member of the community, you're showing that you care. Patients appreciate a doctor who is genuinely invested in their lives and surroundings.

CEO Insight: Being present in your community can significantly enhance trust. Patients don't just want a dentist; they want *their* dentist — someone they know and feel comfortable with.

CEO Story: Dr. Emily's Transition Done Right

When Dr. Emily bought a rural practice, she asked the seller to introduce her at a local health fair. They greeted patients side by side, shaking hands and trading smiles. She retained the front desk receptionist whom everyone loved and mailed a co-signed welcome letter to every household. The result? A 93% patient retention rate and a 20% jump in collections in her first year.

Goodwill Means Trust

Goodwill isn't just about being liked; it's about building trust that lasts beyond the transition of ownership.

- **Patient Trust**: When the outgoing dentist introduces you as their chosen successor, patients often transfer years of loyalty to you almost immediately.

- **Staff Trust**: When the former dentist supports you, the team feels secure that you'll maintain their jobs, culture, and future.

- **Community Trust**: A solid reputation built over years doesn't disappear overnight; it transitions to you as the new owner. This goodwill is what you're truly purchasing when taking over a practice. While the chairs, equipment, and walls hold value, it's the goodwill that often leads to practices selling for more than just their tangible assets.

Why This Matters:

- Likability is about how you come across to people right now.

- Goodwill is about the future; it's the trust that continues even after ownership changes hands. Without goodwill, you're merely acquiring equipment. But with goodwill, you're gaining momentum for your practice's future.

Without goodwill, you're just buying equipment. With goodwill, you're buying momentum.

Life Lesson: The Cost of Neglecting Goodwill: A Practice That Faded Away

I once worked with a young dentist named Dr. Tom, who was eager to buy his first practice. He found a gem in a mid-sized town: $1.1 million in collections, 2,500 active patients, and a seller ready to retire. The price was $875,000, with a net income of $420,000, a solid deal. Tom was thrilled, but he saw the transition as a formality. "I've got this," he told me. "The numbers are great; I don't need the seller hanging around."

Against my advice, Tom negotiated a bare-bones transition: the seller would stay for just two weeks, and there'd be no patient introduction letter. Tom wanted a clean break, confident his clinical skills would win everyone over. The seller, feeling sidelined, agreed but warned, "My patients and staff are loyal to me. You need to ease them into this."

Tom took over, made immediate changes, rebranded, revamped the schedule, and pushed for high-end procedures. Patients felt jarred; the familiar warmth of the practice was gone. The staff, missing the seller's reassurance, grew resentful of the changes. Within six months, 40% of the patients had left for a nearby competitor, and two key hygienists quit. Collections dropped to $700,000, and Tom was struggling to make up the difference in loan payments.

Desperate, Tom called me. "I can't understand it," he said, "the numbers were perfect." I told him: "The numbers were only half the story. You didn't invest in goodwill. You lost the trust that kept this practice alive."

CEO Checklist: Essential Goodwill Moves for Every Buyer

Building trust and goodwill during a transition is crucial. Here's how to create a positive environment as you take the reins:

- **Honor the Seller's Reputation:** Speak kindly about the seller to both staff and patients. Their legacy can be your strongest ally as you establish your own presence.

- **Win Over the Team Early:** Take the time to meet with staff individually. Listen to their goals, frustrations, and ideas. When people feel heard, they're more likely to support new leadership.

- **Protect Continuity:** For the first 90 days, keep schedules, systems, and familiar faces in place. Change can be unsettling; maintaining stability helps build confidence among your team and patients.

- **Secure a Patient Introduction Letter:** A co-signed letter from you and the seller can provide reassurance to patients. It sends a clear message: "You can trust this new doctor—I do."

- **Involve the Seller in the Handoff:** If possible, have the seller introduce you to key patients. A brief endorsement from them can go a long way in establishing trust.

- **Show Humility:** Avoid rushing into rebranding. Take the time to ask questions, observe the existing culture, and respect the established practices before making any changes.

- **Reinforce the Mission:** Clearly communicate your goals at your first team meeting. Emphasize that you are committed to continuing a tradition of high-quality care.

- **Measure Goodwill:** Over your first year, keep an eye on staff retention, patient reappointment rates, and reviews. These metrics serve as a scoreboard for trust and goodwill in your new role.

CEO Insight: Goodwill isn't optional. Ignoring the human side of a transition risks losing what makes a practice special. Build trust, honor the business the seller has created, and invest in people, and you'll create a practice that shines.

Bridging Forward: From Goodwill to Survival

Goodwill earns you the right to sit in the owner's chair, but it doesn't keep you there. Once the ink is dry and the seller steps back, the spotlight shifts entirely to you. Patients expect stability. Staff expect leadership. The community expects continuity.

That's where the first six months matter most. Goodwill opens the door, but systems keep it from slamming shut. In the next chapter, we'll tackle survival and stability head-on: how to protect trust, install systems, and build the foundation that transforms an anxious new owner into a confident CEO.

Executive Summary

1. **Goodwill is Key:** The real value of a practice comes from patient trust, staff loyalty, and community reputation— not just the equipment or location. These elements can make or break a transition.

2. **Smooth Transitions Matter:** Ensuring a seamless transition is vital for retaining patients. Endorsements from the seller, heartfelt letters from patients, and continuity among staff help maintain consistent collections.

3. **Transition Letters Are Essential:** Request or even require a transition letter. A co-signed letter from the seller introducing you and reaffirming their trust can set a positive tone for retaining patients.

4. **Connect with Staff Early On:** Organize a kickoff meeting to share your vision, build rapport, and keep morale high. Meeting with the team early can help everyone feel more comfortable with the changes ahead.

5. **Goodwill Drives Long-Term Growth:** Retaining

patients ensures stability, which in turn fosters growth. Protect your goodwill as if it's your reputation—because it truly is.

Action Plan: Leading like a CEO – Preserving Goodwill with Patients, Staff and Community

1. Protect goodwill. Write down three specific ways you would protect goodwill in the first 90 days after purchase.

2. Build patient trust. If you were a patient, what words or actions from the seller would reassure you that staying with the practice is the right choice?

3. Craft your transition message. Write a short message introducing yourself to the entire team. Express appreciation for their loyalty and your commitment to continuity. Avoid "new sheriff in town" language—build reassurance first, authority second.

4. Protect the culture you inherit. Identify one daily routine, ritual, or practice that defines the team's culture (morning huddle, Friday staff lunches, patient celebrations). Preserve it before you try to improve it.

———————————————————————————

———————————————————————————

———————————————————————————

5. Earn staff buy-in. Identify one step you can take before closing to ensure staff buy-in (e.g., early introductions, team meeting, shared vision).

———————————————————————————

———————————————————————————

———————————————————————————

CEO Toolkit

Download the Goodwill Protection Kit for patient letter templates, staff kickoff meeting guides, and goodwill clauses to include in your LOI at: *www.TransitionOne.net/DentistToCEO/Toolkit*

PART VI: BUILDING YOUR EMPIRE

Chapter 13:
Survival and Systems—
The First 365 Days

Mindset Shift: Year one sets the trajectory. The first six months won't be perfect. They're about survival and systems.

The first six months define everything.

Dr. Kim remembers the moment she signed her first practice loan, her hands trembling with a mix of excitement and anxiety. Just as the ink dried, reality hit her hard: time was of the essence. The waiting room buzzed with patients who were unfamiliar with her, and her staff looked on with skepticism, arms crossed, wondering if she had what it took to lead them. And with every tick of the clock, the weight of that $1.2 million debt loomed larger.

In just 90 days, her patients would form their opinions about her trustworthiness. After six months, her team would decide whether to rally behind her. And within a year, the bank would determine her fate—success or failure.

This is the stark reality of your first year. Those initial months shape your long-term trajectory—establishing your operating systems, financial foundation, and reputation. These aren't merely the early days of ownership; they are the building blocks for the next ten years of your life.

Remember, your first 365 days are less about perfecting your dental skills and more about honing your leadership.

The Four Phases of Ownership

Every new CEO's journey follows four phases:

1. Stabilize (months 1–3): Build trust with patients, staff, and community.

2. Systemize (months 4–6): Create repeatable systems that prevent chaos.

3. Grow (months 7–9): Expand services, visibility, and capacity.

4. Optimize and lead (months 10–12): Strengthen culture, evaluate metrics, and step fully into CEO mode.

This chapter covers Phases 1 & 2: Stabilize and Systemize: the survival half of year one.

Phase 1: Stabilize (months 1–3)

In the early days of your new dental practice, it's all about creating a sense of stability and trust. Whether it's your patients, staff, or even your banker, everyone needs reassurance as you embark on this journey of change.

Transition Checklist for New Dental Practice Owners

The first 90 days are crucial to your success as a practice owner, and knowing how to approach this transition can ease your mind. Focus on building relationships, communicating openly, and maintaining stability to foster goodwill and nurture trust.

Building Patient Trust & Communication

✓ **Send a Co-Signed Transition Letter:** Before Day 1, make sure to send a letter co-signed with the previous owner. This will help ease the minds of your patients.

✓ **Meet the Patients:** Ask the seller to introduce you to patients during their appointments for the first 3–6 months. This personal touch goes a long way.

✓ **Personal Outreach:** Take the time to call your top 50–100 patients personally. This helps you connect and build rapport from the start.

✓ **Open House:** Host a casual open house to welcome your patients and share your story. This is a great opportunity for them to get to know you in a relaxed setting.

✓ **Maintain Consistency:** Keep existing systems, office hours, and billing practices the same during your first 90 days. Familiarity will comfort your patients.

For example, Dr. James successfully took over a practice with 2,500 patients by focusing on connection. He sent heartfelt letters, received introductions from the seller, and hosted a "Meet the Doctor" open house. This approach led to an impressive 94% retention rate of existing patients and the addition of 200 new patients in his first year!

Pro Tip: A simple five-minute personal phone call to your top patients can create more loyalty than an expensive $10,000 marketing campaign. Building that personal connection is invaluable!

Connecting with Your Team

Take the time to sit down one-on-one with each team member. This is your chance to really understand their roles and listen to any concerns they might have.

✓ Kick things off with a Day 1 meeting! Share your vision and reassure everyone about their job security.

✓ During your first 90 days, try to avoid making any big changes to pay, schedules, or responsibilities. Stability is key as you settle in.

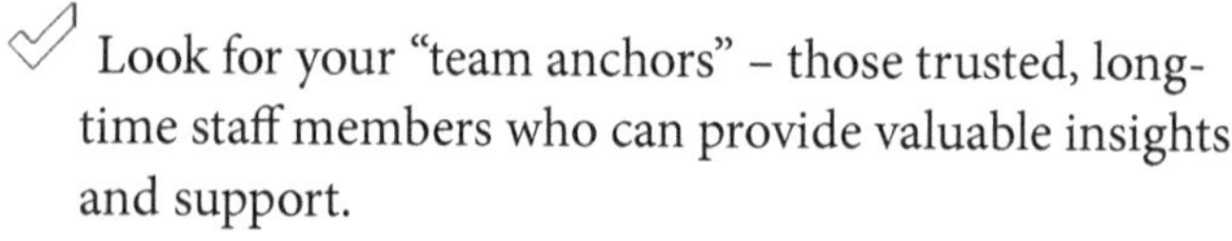

Look for your "team anchors" – those trusted, long-time staff members who can provide valuable insights and support.

Encourage your team to share their ideas for improving efficiency, and make it a point to act on at least one suggestion quickly.

Mindset Shift: Your staff are your partners in success. By earning their trust, you'll cultivate loyalty that truly makes a difference.

Seller Support

Ensure the seller is available: The seller should be committed to working with you for 1–2 days a week for 3–6 months after the sale.

Set clear expectations: Have an open conversation with the seller about what kind of public support and private mentorship you can expect.

Encourage involvement: Invite the seller to join team or patient meetings to help with the transition.

Life Lesson: The Risk that Almost Cost Everything

I once worked with a dentist named Dr. Sarah, a brilliant clinician with a fire to succeed. She bought a 6-operatory practice in a tight-knit town: $1 million in collections, 2,600 active patients, and a net income of $400,000. The seller agreed to a six-month transition, and Sarah was poised for greatness. But in her excitement to make the practice her own, she moved too fast and nearly lost everything.

Sarah wanted to "modernize" immediately. On day one, she changed the scheduling software, redesigned the waiting room, and pushed for cosmetic procedures the practice hadn't offered. She skipped the patient transition letter, assuming her skills would win everyone over. The seller, present only sparingly, couldn't bridge the gap. Patients felt unsettled by the rapid changes; many missed the familiar routines. The staff, blind-sided by new systems, grew frustrated. By month three, patient retention dropped to 75%, and two hygienists quit.

Sarah called me in a panic. "I thought I was improving things," she said. "Now it's falling apart."

We sat down and mapped out a reset: Sarah reinstated the old scheduling system, sent a warm and welcoming transition letter with the seller's endorsement and held a staff meeting to apologize and listen. She leaned on the seller for more patient introductions and hosted a community open house. Slowly, trust returned. By year two, Sarah had rebuilt retention to 90% and grown collections to $1.2 million.

Pro Tip: Before you change the space, prove you won't change the standards. When schedules stay steady, paychecks arrive on time, and leadership feels predictable, trust follows long before any renovation does.

Phase 2: Systemize (months 4–6)

Simply surviving isn't enough to help your practice thrive. After establishing trust, it's time to focus on systemizing your operations.

Strong systems do more than just improve efficiency—they give you back precious time to lead. Without effective systems in place, you may find yourself constantly putting out fires, leaving little room for leadership. On the other hand, when you have solid systems, you can step back to mentor your team, invest in their growth, and think strategically like a CEO instead of just reacting like an employee. With standardized workflows and clear responsibilities, you reclaim the most valuable asset of leadership: time. This newfound time allows you to coach a hygienist, support a new assistant, and focus on the bigger picture.

Here's what you can do:

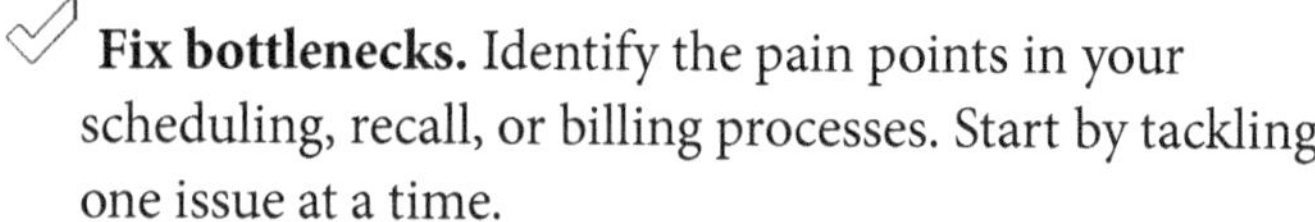

- **Fix bottlenecks.** Identify the pain points in your scheduling, recall, or billing processes. Start by tackling one issue at a time.

- **Delegate and empower.** Clearly assign ownership of tasks to your team members, allowing them to take charge of their responsibilities.

 **Schedule weekly huddles.** Hold brief 30-minute meetings to review key metrics and ensure everyone is aligned and on the same page.

 **Audit overhead.** Regularly evaluate your payroll, supplies, and rent against industry benchmarks. Make adjustments early to avoid unnecessary strain.

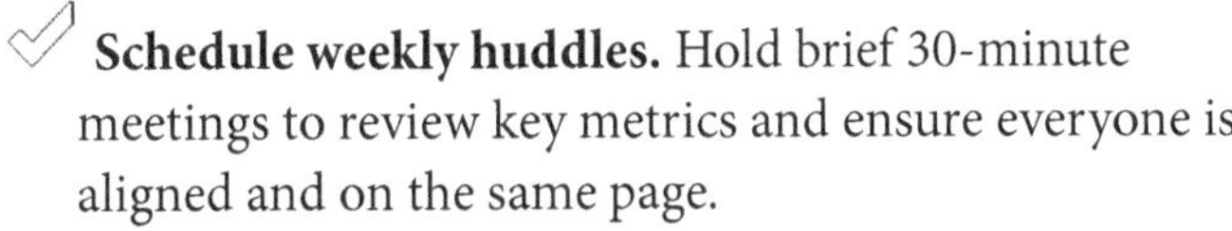

CEO Insight: Remember, chaos can multiply as your practice grows, leading to potential disaster. But with effective systems in place, growth can be a pathway to success.

CEO Story: Dr. Dan is a powerful example of how stability and systems can unlock value without a major overhaul. In his first six months of ownership, he focused on strengthening patient recall, introducing an automated reminder and scheduling system that drove a sharp increase in hygiene visits—and, in turn, restorative procedures. Within a year, collections climbed from $1.3M to $1.8M, net margin reached 41%, and he reduced to four clinical days, reserving Fridays for dedicated CEO time.

His banker called him "the safest borrower I've ever seen." His staff called it "the best year we've ever had." His wife called it "the life we dreamed about."

That's what the first six months can do. They don't just stabilize your practice; they unlock your future.

Financial Reality Check #6: The Cost of Inefficiency

Let's take a moment to reflect on the true financial impact of inefficiency in our operations. Here's what the numbers reveal:

Operational Leak	Daily Loss	Annual Loss (based on 240 workdays)
4 missed hygiene appointments per day	$600	$144,000
2 hours of unfilled doctor appointments per week	$1,000	$48,000
3% of uncollected accounts receivable on $1 million in collections	–	$30,000

Total Hidden Cost of Inefficiency: Approximately $220,000 per year.

These figures are based on a practice operating with a revenue of $1 million over 240 working days a year. It's important to recognize how these inefficiencies can add up and impact our bottom line significantly. By addressing these areas, we can work towards a more efficient and profitable practice.

What to Track by Month Six

The first six months aren't about explosive growth—they're about proving the foundation is solid. These metrics tell you whether the transition worked or whether cracks are forming beneath the surface.

Patient Retention — Target: 90%+

What it means: At least 90% of the patients who were active at acquisition are still scheduling, showing up, and accepting care.

How to track it:

- Compare active patient counts at closing vs. month six

- Use a consistent definition (typically 18-month active patients)

- Watch recall reappointment rates and cancellation patterns

Why it matters: Patients don't leave because of new ownership; they leave because of uncertainty. If retention drops below 90%, it usually signals breakdowns in communication, trust, or front-desk execution.

Staff Retention – Target: 90%+

What it means: At least 90% of the original team remains employed six months after closing.

How to track it:

- Count voluntary vs. involuntary departures

- Pay special attention to hygienists and front-desk staff

- Track overtime and sick days as early warning signs

Why it matters: Staff continuity preserves patient confidence and operational rhythm. Early turnover creates downstream issues in scheduling, collections, and morale that are expensive to fix later.

Collections — Target: +10% Trend

What it means: Collections should be trending upward by at least 10% compared to the pre-acquisition baseline—not from price hikes, but from better execution.

How to track it:

- Monthly rolling collections vs. same-month pre-close

- Separate production growth from collection efficiency

- Monitor AR aging alongside gross collections

Why it matters: A healthy upward trend signals that systems are stabilizing, patients are accepting care, and the team is aligned with your expectations.

Hygiene as a % of Production — Target: 25–30%

What it means: Hygiene should contribute roughly one-quarter to one-third of total production.

How to track it:

- Monthly hygiene production ÷ total practice production

- Monitor reappointment rates and hygiene fill rates

- Watch hygiene capacity vs. actual utilization

Why it matters: Hygiene is the engine of predictable cash flow and diagnosis. Underperformance here usually points to recall leakage, scheduling gaps, or poor patient handoffs.

Overhead — Target: ≤60% of Collections

What it means: Total operating expenses (excluding owner compensation and debt service) should stay at or below 60% of collections.

How to track it:

- Monthly P&L with normalized categories

- Isolate payroll, supplies, and lab as the big three

- Watch for creeping "small" expenses that add up

Why it matters: Overhead discipline gives you margin. Margin gives you options—for raises, marketing, equipment, and growth. Once overhead drifts, everything feels tight—even in a busy practice.

Why the First Six Months Matter

The initial six months are about stability, not speed:

- Building trust with patients and staff

- Installing discipline in scheduling, billing, and reporting

- Creating order where uncertainty once lived

Hit these benchmarks, and you're no longer "the new owner." You're the leader of a stable business.

What Changes After Month Six

Once stability is proven, the strategy shifts.

Now you can:

- Invest confidently in growth initiatives

- Expand hygiene and doctor capacity

- Increase marketing without fear

- Optimize systems instead of firefighting

Growth only works when the foundation holds. Month six is where you find out if it does.

CEO Insight: The first 180 days won't make you rich, but they will ensure you're ready for what's next. Being prepared is key to growing in a controlled manner rather than getting swept up in chaos.

Executive Summary – Survival and Systems

1. **The first six months define the next ten years**. Patients, staff, and even lenders are judging your leadership long before they judge your dentistry. Win trust first.

2. **Stability before strategy**. Don't overhaul systems too early. Keep what works intact for 90 days while you build confidence with staff and patients.

3. **Culture compounds**. Meet with every team member one-on-one. The loyalty and morale you build now become the fuel for growth later.

4. **Systems mean sanity**. Document workflows, fix one bottleneck at a time, and install weekly huddles. Chaos times growth equals disaster.

5. **Trust is transferable**. Lean on the seller to co-sign patient letters, endorse you publicly, and mentor you privately. Their goodwill is the bridge to your credibility.

6. **Cash, culture, capacity, clarity**. These are the four anchors of your first six months. Master them and you'll walk into the growth phase with confidence.

Action Plan

1. Document one system at a time. Identify your three most inconsistent areas of the new practice. (example: scheduling, billing, hygiene recall). Pick one per quarter and create a simple written or video standard operating procedure (SOP) that anyone could follow.

    ____

    ____

    ____

2. Strengthen cash discipline. Set a cash discipline goal for the first six months (e.g., track weekly deposits, build 2–3 months of reserves).

    ____

    ____

    ____

3. Define your 180-day benchmarks. Write down your 180-day benchmarks (percentage of patient retention, staff retention, collections growth, hygiene, overhead). Keep them posted where you'll see them weekly.

    ____

    ____

    ____

CEO Toolkit

Download the First-Year CEO Operating System—a suite of templates including the Weekly CEO Huddle Agenda, Cash Flow Tracker, and System Documentation Checklist to help you stabilize your practice and lead with clarity at: *www.TransitionOne.net/DentistToCEO/Toolkit*

Chapter 14: Growth Without Burnout

The Alarm Clock Moment

Dr. Marisa sat in her car at 8 p.m., engine off, forehead pressed against the steering wheel. Forty-eight straight clinical days. Her assistants were exhausted, hygiene was double-booked, and collections were climbing—but her energy was gone. She didn't need another production goal. She needed a plan to breathe.

That's the real story behind growth. It's about building systems that serve your life, not consume it.

The Turn: What Growth Really Means

The hardest truth every owner learns is that burnout doesn't come from overwork, it comes from misalignment. You can work 50 hours a week and feel alive, or 30 hours and feel buried. The difference? Whether your hours serve your vision or just your calendar.

That's the 180° turn—the moment you stop chasing more and start building better.

The Contrast: Two Kinds of Growth

Imagine two practices. Both start the year at $1M in collections.

Practice A adds more hours, hires more staff, launches new services, and doubles its marketing budget. Collections rise 20% but so do expenses. Profits barely move. The staff is exhausted.

Practice B fixes one bottleneck, improves recall, and trains the team on a new system. Collections rise 10% with no extra overhead. Profits soar. The staff feels energized, not drained.

Both grew. Only one grew smarter.

From Stability to Scale

In Chapter 13, we discussed how to build a foundation: survival and systems. After month six, you've stabilized patient trust, rallied your team, leaned on the seller, and installed systems that turned chaos into order. That gave you credibility. That gave you trust.

Now comes the next six months. This is where you shift gears from stabilizing to scaling, from systems to strategy. But here's the catch: growth doesn't mean doing more of everything. It means doing more of the right things.

The Four Phases of Ownership: Your Roadmap to Freedom

Phase	Months	Core Focus	Primary Goal	CEO Mindset
1. Stabilize	1-3	Build trust with patients and team	Preserve goodwill and cash flow	"Earn trust before making change."
2. Systemize	4-6	Create repeatable processes and metrics	Replace chaos with consistency	"Document it once so you don't redo it twice."
3. Grow	7-9	Expand services and visibility strategically	Add revenue without burnout	"Do more of what works best, not everything."
4. Optimize	10-12	Refine systems and develop leaders	Scale profit and culture in sync	"Lead people, not production."

Each phase builds on the previous one— survival becomes stability, stability can help the practice scale, and scale guides you to freedom.

Phase 3: Growth (months 7–9)

Once stability and systems are locked in, you can finally add weight.

✓ Expand services strategically. Choose one service (Invisalign, implants, sleep dentistry) based on patient demand. Market it intentionally, not frantically.

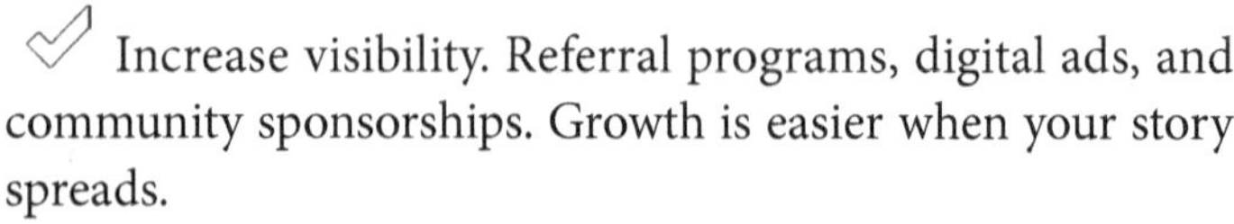 Increase visibility. Referral programs, digital ads, and community sponsorships. Growth is easier when your story spreads.

✓ Upgrade technology. Add one high-impact tool (digital X-rays, intraoral scanner) that boosts efficiency and the patient experience.

✓ Strengthen team roles. With systems in place, train staff on higher-value responsibilities so growth doesn't bottleneck at you.

Case snapshot: Dr. Lewis added implants in month nine. The result? $200K growth in revenue with no added ops. That's smart growth.

Phase 4: Optimize and Lead (Months 10–12)

As you enter the final phase of your first year, it's not about seeking more; it's about fine-tuning what's already working, leading with clarity, and building momentum that will carry you smoothly into Year Two.

Key Moves to Cement Your Momentum

✓ Review Performance Metrics: Take a close look at how your practice is performing compared to the benchmarks established in earlier chapters. Aim for at least 40% net income, over 2,000 active patients, and $600–$700 in revenue per patient.

 Invest in Your Team: Focus on ongoing training, cross-training, and leadership development. Remember, growth can be fragile, so a strong team is essential.

Build Office Culture Rituals: Create weekly huddles, celebrate quarterly milestones, and implement recognition rewards. A thriving culture keeps the momentum alive and your team engaged.

Protect Your Time as CEO: Set aside a few hours each week for strategic planning. By this stage, you've evolved from being just a dentist to being the CEO of your practice.

CEO Insight: Surviving proves you can run a practice; optimizing it shows you can lead one.

Growth Without Burnout

Growth doesn't fail because of ambition. It fails because owners add complexity faster than their systems and their people can handle. This list isn't about accelerating growth. It's about **protecting momentum** so growth doesn't turn into exhaustion.

1. Optimize Operations: Streamline processes with cloud-based billing, hold weekly huddles, and delegate vendor negotiations to save time and stress.

2. Expand Services Wisely: Consider adding one new service that meets patient demand and has a clear return on

investment.

3. Strengthen Community Connections: Get involved by sponsoring an event, joining a civic group, or hosting an open house to build your practice's presence in the community.

4. Protect Your Team: Keep an eye on staff turnover, morale, and training opportunities. Rapid growth without team buy-in can lead to chaos.

5. Guard Your Profitability: Be cautious not to pursue top-line growth at the expense of your net margins. Balance is key.

CEO Freedom Metrics Recap

Freedom isn't a feeling—it's measurable. These are the benchmarks that tell you you're no longer just running a practice, you're leading a business that runs itself.

Metric	Target Range	What It Means
Net Margin	≥ 40 %	Your business generates true profit after overhead—not just revenue.
Overhead	≤ 60 % of collections	Your systems and discipline protect your bottom line.
CEO Time	≥ 2 hrs per week dedicated to leadership, strategy, and systems	You're not trapped in the chair—you're leading from it.
Cash Reserve	2–3 months of fixed expenses	You own control of your time and decisions—not the bank.

Metric	Target Range	What It Means
Team Retention	≥ 85 % year-over-year	Your culture compounds—people stay because they grow with you.

CEO Insight: Freedom has a formula.

When your profit, people, and time align, ownership stops being stressful and starts being sustainable.

Life Lesson: Dr. Carl's Growth Gamble

Dr. Carl walked into his new 10-op practice like a man on a mission. With $1.9 million in collections and 4,400 active patients, it was everything he'd dreamed of. He didn't just want to run it—he wanted to scale it to the moon.

"Two years," he told me. "I'll double this place in two years." Six months later, the dream started to unravel.

Dr. Carl had borrowed another $150,000 for a glossy marketing blitz and a shiny 3D cone beam machine. He rolled out new services overnight (implants, ortho, the works) and hired an associate to handle the patient surge he was sure was coming. But the surge never came.

The $150K campaign brought in only 50 new patients. The associate sat idle, draining $100K in salary. The team was overwhelmed, stumbling through procedures they weren't trained for. Patients noticed. Complaints trickled in. Collections slid from $1.9M to $1.5M in less than a year.

That's when Carl called me, voice heavy with frustration. "I thought more was better," he admitted. "Now I'm bleeding cash."

We hit reset. Carl shelved the ortho services, retrained his staff, and focused on one growth lever: implants. He ran a simple recall program, reactivated lapsed patients, and built momentum locally. Eighteen months later, his practice wasn't just surviving, it was thriving at $2.1 million in collections.

Carl's takeaway? "I tried to grow too fast without a plan. If I'd listened to my patients and my team, I would've saved myself a fortune."

Year One CEO Dashboard

By the end of Year One, your practice should demonstrate stability, discipline, and controlled momentum. This dashboard is your scorecard—not to impress anyone, but to confirm you've built something durable.

Core Stability Metrics

Metric	Target by Month 12	What It Confirms
Patient Retention	90%+	Patients trust the transition and accept your leadership
Staff Retention	90%+	The team feels safe, valued, and aligned
Collections Growth	+10–15% over baseline	Systems are working, not just effort
Hygiene % of Revenue	25–30%	Recall, diagnosis, and scheduling discipline
Overhead	≤60% of collections	Margin discipline and operational control
CEO Time	≥2 hours/week	You're leading the business—not trapped in it

How to Use This Dashboard

- Review monthly, not emotionally

- Track trends, not isolated months

- Address misses early—small drifts become big problems

Growth doesn't happen because of luck. It occurs after a series of disciplined choices stacked on the systems you built in Chapter 13.

CEO Insight: The Math of Freedom

Every 1% drop in overhead becomes one extra week of profit each year.

Every 5% improvement in hygiene recall becomes one extra month of free cash flow.

Growth is measured in time, not just dollars.

Translation: The smarter your systems run, the more weeks of freedom you earn back.

Victory Story: Dr. Maria's Strategic Growth

Dr. Maria Lopez purchased a $1.1M practice with 2,200 active patients. Like most new owners, she was tempted to sprint: new equipment, expanded hours, splashy marketing campaigns. But instead, she chose discipline.

Her first priority was systems, not services. She tightened hygiene recall, introduced morning huddles, and tied staff bonuses to reappointment rates. Within three months, her patient retention rate jumped from 82% to 92%.

Only then did she expand. At month seven, Maria added Invisalign as a new service, but she rolled it out with intention: CE training for her team, a simple in-office promotion, and a patient education night. No chaos, no overwhelm.

She didn't add hours or staff until utilization hit 85%. When she did, it was strategic, one new assistant, one upgraded scanner, both timed to match demand.

By the end of Year One:

- collections climbed from $1.1M to $1.5M,

- net margins held steady at 40%,

- staff described the culture as "the most supportive and energizing it's ever been,

- Patients were referring friends and family.

Her banker called her "a textbook case of disciplined growth." Her team called her "the best leader we've had."

Pro Tip: Growth done right doesn't feel frantic. It feels focused. Maria didn't grow by doing more; she grew by doing the right things in the right order.

The Final Word: From Dentist to CEO

Make no mistake: You are being watched.

Patients are watching—deciding whether you are the doctor they will trust for decades. Staff are watching—deciding whether you are the leader worth committing their careers to. Your lender is watching—deciding whether this deal becomes a quiet success story or a cautionary tale.

Yes, the numbers matter. But numbers alone don't build enduring practices. What truly matters is leadership. It's the culture you create. It's the systems you put in place.

When you treat your practice as a thriving business rather than just a paycheck— something significant shifts. You stop seeing yourself merely as a dentist. You start building your vision as a CEO.

This book doesn't offer shortcuts. Instead, it provides you with a framework—a new way to think, decide, and lead.

You now hold the roadmap in your hands. The responsibility is yours. From this point on, you're not just practicing dentistry. You're creating something that will endure.

This book gave you the playbook. Now it's your move.

Executive Summary

---

1. **Growth shouldn't be rushed; make it strategic.** Scale what works, not everything at once.

2. **Phase 3 is expansion**: add services, visibility, and tech with intention

3. **Phase 4 is optimization**: refine metrics, invest in people, and protect culture

4. **Burnout comes from unmanaged growth**: avoid it with systems, focus, and CEO time.

5. **By year the end of year one, you're not just surviving**. You're leading a million-dollar practice with momentum.

Action Plan: Growth without Burnout

1. Redefine growth on your terms. Write down what growth truly means for you this year: more profit, more time freedom, stronger culture, or selective expansion. Clear emotional goals keep your growth aligned with purpose, not pressure.

____

____

2. Identify one scalable service. Review your production by procedure and pinpoint one area with consistent demand and healthy margins (e.g., clear aligners, implants, or same-day crowns). Build a system to expand it without overloading your team.

____

____

3. Audit your operations for efficiency this week. Evaluate scheduling, team roles, and workflows. Eliminate one

duplication, one bottleneck, or energy drain. True growth comes from tightening before adding.

____

____

____

4. Protect the culture that got you here. As volume increases, burnout can hide in communication gaps. Schedule a monthly culture check-in with the team. Celebrate small wins and reinforce your mission with praise so growth strengthens morale not stress.

____

____

____

CEO Toolkit

Download the Sustainable Growth Blueprint—a strategic worksheet with tools to track profit per procedure, assess team capacity, and build a balanced growth plan that scales income and impact without sacrificing your sanity at: _www.TransitionOne.net/DentistToCEO/Toolkit_

Epilogue:
Your CEO Future Starts Now

The office is dark again. But this time, it's yours. The monitor's glow still cuts through the night—only now, it reflects your logo, your name, your numbers. You started this journey staring at a screen that belonged to someone else. Now the glow you see isn't from another dentist's computer, it's from your own sign lit up in the dark.

Every dentist who steps off the associate treadmill faces the same line—comfort on one side, control on the other. Most people don't fail to cross it because they're incapable. They don't cross it because waiting feels safer than deciding. But once you see the math, the patterns, and the stakes, indecision stops being neutral.

You don't need another degree, another promise, or anyone's approval. You need a decision.

Because once you bet on yourself, every patient, every staff meeting, every system, and every number becomes part of a business you own. That's when growth stops feeling like burnout with nowhere to go and starts feeling like freedom. So wherever you are tonight, maybe staring at that same glow, remember this: the line is real.

And from here on out, which side you live on is yours to own.

Author's Note

Over the past decade, I've watched hundreds of dentists transform from exhausted associates into confident CEOs. That's why I built the Dentist to CEO community—a place for owners and future owners to share tools, metrics, and mentorship that make the journey lighter and faster.

You can download every worksheet, checklist, and dashboard mentioned in this book—and join our growing network of entrepreneurial dentists—at *www.TransitionOne.net/Dentist-ToCEO*.

Appendix:
Tools, Templates & Checklists

Your journey from dentist to CEO doesn't end here. This appendix is your vault of every worksheet, checklist, and calculator referenced in this book, designed to help you buy, grow, and lead with confidence.

Access Everything Online: *www.TransitionOne.net/Dentist-ToCEO/Toolkit*

Each downloadable file is updated regularly with the newest versions used by our TransitionOne clients.

Contracts and Legal

Protect yourself before you sign. These tools help you negotiate smarter, spot red flags, and secure fair terms that protect both your paycheck and your potential.

- Associate Contract Checklist

- Letter of Intent Toolkit

- Sample Asset Purchase Agreement Clauses

- Noncompete Negotiation Playbook

- Transition Timeline Template; a 6-month roadmap to plan communication, team meetings, and patient letters before and after closing.

Financials and Valuation

Decode the numbers that drive every practice. Use these scorecards and calculators to value, compare, and forecast like a CEO.

- Practice Evaluation Scorecard

- Financial Due Diligence Checklist

- EBITDA & Add-Back Worksheet

- Loan Comparison Calculator

- CEO Performance Scorecard – track collections, overhead, hygiene %, staff retention, and profit quarterly to measure your growth as a CEO.

Operations and Leadership

Lead your team with clarity and structure. These templates help you systemize workflows, align communication, and stabilize culture through transition.

- Patient Transition Letter Template

- First-Week Operational Roadmap

- 100-Day CEO Integration Plan

- Staff Onboarding & Culture Checklist

Growth and Strategy

Scale strategically. Use these planners and dashboards to identify growth levers, improve efficiency, and prepare for expansion or exit.

- 12-Month Growth Strategy Planner

- Marketing ROI Tracker

- Overhead Optimization Worksheet

- Exit Planning Starter Kit

How to Use this Toolkit

Print it. Test it. Refine it. These tools are living documents—built to evolve with your practice, your systems, and your leadership.

CEO Insight: Every great practice starts with a plan. These tools are yours—use them, adapt them, and keep building the business and life you were meant to own.

Glossary and Key Concepts

Financial Metrics

Accounts Receivable (A/R): Unpaid services billed to patients or insurance. In dentistry, patients are typically expected to pay their bill within 30 days. If you request an A/R report from a practice and find that a significant portion is older than 30 days, it's worth digging deeper. Past-due A/R can signal issues with collections, billing processes, or patient communication. It's also an opportunity to update systems to make repayment easier and faster—improving cash flow, reducing bad debt risk, and getting money back to the business more efficiently.

Cash Flow: Net income plus add-backs—money available to cover debt, pay the owner, and reinvest in the practice.

Collections: Actual revenue received after insurance adjustments (not just billed production).

Cost Per Patient: Purchase price divided by active patients. Target: $300–$500. Red flag if cost is above $700 per patient.

EBITDA: Earnings Before Interest, Taxes, Depreciation, and Amortization. Industry standard measure of profitability.

Family or Related Party Expenses: Payments to family members that aren't necessary for operations.

Net Income: Profit after expenses. Target: 35–40%+ of collections.

Non-Cash Expenses: Depreciation, amortization, or other accounting entries that don't impact cash.

Non-Essential Personal Expenses: Owner's personal spending run through the practice, e.g., personal travel, car payments, or memberships.

Normalized Expenses / Add-backs: Expenses added back to net income to reflect the true earning potential of the practice. Common types include:

One-Time Expenses: Non-recurring costs like legal fees, consulting, or renovations.

Owner's Compensation: Salary, bonuses, and benefits paid to the current owner.

Overhead Percentage: Operating expenses ÷ collections. Healthy range: ≤ 60%.

Working Capital: Funds set aside for initial expenses such as payroll, supplies, and overhead after closing.

Deal Terms

- **Asset Purchase Agreement (APA):** Binding contract detailing all tangible and intangible assets transferred in the sale.

- **Goodwill:** Intangible value—reputation, staff loyalty, and patient trust. Often 80–90% of total sale price.

- **Letter of Intent (LOI):** Non-binding agreement outlining purchase terms. Serves as a roadmap for the purchase agreement.

- **Restrictive Covenant / Noncompete:** Contract clause that limits where a dentist can practice post-employment.

- **SBA Loan:** Government-backed loan (typically 7a program) with favorable terms, used for practice acquisition.

- **Seller Financing:** When the seller funds part of the sale, often through a promissory note, to bridge valuation gaps.

- **Side Agreement:** Additional agreement outside the main Asset Purchase Agreement (APA), often for A/R, equipment, or employment.

Practice Health Metrics

- **400-Patient Rule:** 400 active patients = one doctor day per week of demand.

- **Active Patients:** Patients seen at least once in the last 18 months. Core measure of practice vitality and revenue potential.

- **Case Acceptance Rate:** 70–80 % of diagnosed treatment accepted.

- **Clinical Supplies (5–7%):** Should stay predictable; spikes often point to poor ordering systems or excessive waste.

- **Doctor Production per Day:** $4 K–$6 K/day average for general dentistry.

- **Hygiene Production %:** Hygiene department should generate 25–30% of total practice revenue. This signals strong patient retention, a full schedule, predictable and recurring income, and a healthy pipeline for ongoing growth.

- **Lab Fees** (6–8%): Can rise with cosmetic or specialty work—make sure fee schedules account for lab-heavy procedures.

- **Marketing** (2–4%): Necessary for growth, but overspending rarely produces proportional results, track ROI closely.

- **New Patient Flow:** Number of new patients per month. Benchmark: 20–25+ for steady growth.

- **Office/Admin** (1–2%): Often overlooked, but recurring subscriptions and office services can bloat this line if unchecked.

- **Patient Retention Rate:** ≥ 90 % returning annually—core indicator of goodwill strength.

- **Rent** (4–6% of collections): Higher than this can squeeze margins, especially in older buildings or high-rent districts.

- **Staff Retention Rate:** ≥ 85 % year-over-year. Culture continuity protects profitability.

- **Staff Wages & Benefits** (28–33%): Biggest overhead category, watch for overstaffing or costly benefit packages that creep above target.

- **Utilities & Misc** (1-2%): Small, but a good indicator of how tightly the office controls overhead.

Acknowledgements

The insights in this book are the culmination of years of experience, made possible by the people who stood by me, challenged me, and inspired me to think bigger, serve better, and lead boldly.

First and foremost, to my incredible wife, Sophia, your patience, love, and unwavering belief in me have been the bedrock of every bold step I've taken. You've been my steady hand through every late night, big idea, and unexpected turn.

To my sons, Christopher and Chandler, you are the pride of my life. Watching you grow into disciplined, driven young men has been one of my greatest joys. Thank you for reminding me what achievement really means.

To my mother, your strength, sacrifice, and unconditional love gave me the foundation to dream big and work hard. Every opportunity I've chased, every obstacle I've overcome, and every success I've celebrated is rooted in the values you instilled in me. Thank you for being my first teacher, and my biggest cheerleader.

To my brother, Jared Dillian, your insights, intellect, and support have shaped my thinking and challenged me to raise the bar in all things business and life.

To the TransitionOne team, Ingrid Beavers, Kelly Salvatore, Todd Blackmar, and Greg Wetzel: thank you for being the kind of teammates that elevate this mission beyond transactions. You've helped transform practice transitions into life-changing opportunities for the dentists we serve and I'm proud to build this with you.

To my inspirational friends who are like family: Jordan Houseman, Cody Chaffee, Preston Doty and especially Dr. Todd Russell: your wisdom, leadership, and encouragement have left a permanent mark on my journey. Your examples continue to inspire the next generation of dental entrepreneurs.

And finally, to every young dentist reading this, this book was written with you in mind. Your dreams, your drive, and your courage to take the leap are what keep me passionate about this work. Keep betting on yourself, your future is waiting.

With deep gratitude,

Chris K. Vandiford

About the Author

Chris Vandiford is a nationally recognized transition advisor and founder of TransitionOne, a premier firm guiding dentists from associate roles to confident practice ownership. With over 600+ successful transitions under his belt, Chris is known for turning complex deals into clear, empowering journeys for first-time buyers, seasoned sellers, and entrepreneurial leaders alike.

His signature approach combines real-world deal experience, battle-tested leadership principles, and a deep respect for the human side of practice ownership.

Through live trainings, dental school lectures, and national conference keynotes, Chris has become a trusted voice for those ready to think like CEOs, not just clinicians. His work is featured in mastermind groups, online platforms, and private coaching sessions for dentists serious about growth.

He is also the founder of DDS Refinance, a lending advisory firm for practice buyers and owners seeking smarter loan structures.

Chris lives in Ohio with his wife Sophia, where he balances business with family, faith, and a few too many whiteboards.